DATA SCIENCE
IN HIGHER EDUCATION

DATA SCIENCE
IN HIGHER EDUCATION

*Step-by-Step Machine Learning
for Institutional Researchers*

Published in Chico, CA
ISBN: 1515206467
ISBN-13: 978-1515206460

Disclaimer. Since you're using computer code in this book, it goes without saying that I am not responsible for anything you do (or fail to do) by following along in this book. Further, I am not liable for any result, intended or otherwise, that comes from your using the concepts and/or code from this book. While I have tried to make every effort to ensure that the code presented herein is accurate, changes are made to third-party packages all the time and I am not responsible for any code in this book no longer working or failing to perform as expected.

Questions and Comments. Please feel free to send me your questions and comments via email (jesse@lawsonry.com). Any changes to the book that are a result of our email discussions will result in you being credited appropriately on the Special Thanks page.

CONTENTS

For Sami, who never did (and still doesn't) get frustrated with my self-imposed deadlines

Special Thanks

Jorge Sanchez, for our lengthy sociological discussions in your research office; Aeron Zentner, for introducing me to institutional effectiveness and planning; Jerry Halverson, for being a supportive and helpful mentor in the classes I had with you; Lori Kelly, for helping to shape me in my first sociology class in college; James Henslin, for your introductory book on sociology that was responsible for me wanting to change my major. All of you have helped me discover my passion for working in public education.

A Very Special Thanks to Mark Storer, my high school English teacher. In addition to cautioning that I'll "never make it as a long-hander," and that if I wanted to be a writer that I should just shut up and write, you demonstrated, through tenacity, discipline, humor, and grit, how to be a critical thinker. Your classes inspired me to write and self-reflect and I'll never forget you for that.

"Once man turned their thinking over to machines in the hope that this would set them free. But that only permitted other men with machines to enslave them."

–Frank Herbert, *Dune*

ABOUT THIS BOOK

Data Science in Higher Education is not your average book on analytics. Instead of giving you a list of tools sorted by chapter and then using some default datasets that every book on the subject uses, we're going to use real educational data from real institutions (whose identities have been omitted) to create real predictive models. I've tweaked the circumstances of how I came to acquire the data a bit, which is precisely how this book is different from other books. Instead of a list of tools, we start with a problem (in the form of a case study) and then use a particular tool to solve it. I have yet to find a resource for institutional researchers that does this, but if you know of one or if one is published after this book is, please send me an email and tell me so I can include it in this section.

Chapter 1

INTRODUCTION

I had been consulting with institutions across the country for a few years before finally taking a job at a community college in 2014. What I discovered early on is that higher education —*community colleges* in particular —are lacking in internal research effectiveness, and not for a lack of effort. In fact, the researchers I have talked to over the years have time and time again expressed the same frustrations with higher education as a whole:

- Technology and research staff are underfunded, yet are the backbone of most (if not all) institutional operations and decisions

- Research offices only have a few people and are bogged down with report generation rather than actual research

- When actual research is able to take place, overly simplistic methods (like frequency analysis with pie and bar charts) are favored over more robust (and accurate) methods.

Adding to their frustrations are hundreds of thousands of grant dollars that are often spent on expensive, well-marketed technology products instead of being invested in the process of institutional optimization and change. This was incredibly concerning for me, but when I spoke out at a student success conference in California one year I got a more clear picture of what was going on.

"The problem," one director of research was telling me, "is that institutions don't listen to researchers or any of the data people because they're talking in terms that they don't understand. Do you think the president or vice presidents care about which statistical validation test you used to come up with whatever you found? No, they don't. They're in the same boat as for-profit company leaders: show us a model that will accurately predict behavior so that we can make more money."

And so began my journey to understand how colleges and universities were thinking more like the private sector in how they approached their decision-making processes. What I found early on was that predictive analytics was at the forefront of college enrollment and retention research, with a few institutions employing very expensive modeling software from big companies promising growth and prosperity. When I looked to non-academic material for teaching data science, I found a lot of material on business-oriented analytics but nothing specific to higher education. In fact, in teaching machine learning through my online classes I realized that I spent a great deal of time translating business analytics knowledge over to higher education. On top of that, the books that I would use in my classes would pack in so much information that it was often hard for researchers to develop intuition in such a short time (who has time to sit around and read a textbook these days? I don't know about you, but I have a four year old and twin one year olds; I don't have time to study a textbook right now!)

So I sought out to develop a course that was approachable, something that researchers could dive into and immediately relate to. This of course turned into a huge project and eventually the people I shared my ideas with said that it might be better suited for a book. As you can see, I agreed with them.

THE BIG QUESTION

Leaders in higher education have demonstrated time and time again that data science is a key driver for institutional effectiveness. When colleges and universities hear about the successful employment of trending strategies like big data mining and predictive analytics, decision makers often come together to determine the ability of their own institution to adopt third-party or even roll out their own analysis operations. After the initial excitement over the possibilities that data science has to offer, however, decision-makers are faced with several internal obstacles.

According to EduCause, the three major concerns about the growing use of analytics in higher education are Affordability, Misuse of Data, and Regulations Requiring Use of Data. These are closely followed by concerns about whether Higher Education even knows how to use data to make decision-making and whether data collected is accurate or not. All of these concerns can be summarized in one concise sentence (that I call the Big Question):

Can we afford to do data analysis, and if we can, how do we know we're doing it right?

To mitigate the first half —whether the institution can afford data analytics or not —is a matter of opportunity cost; what is the opportunity cost of not cleaning, mining, testing, and deploying models based off of the enormous amount of data that institutions college nowadays? As one anonymous institutional researcher points out, "it is very expensive to bring a student to campus who's not going to succeed, and so you have to be doing things all the way along the line to make sure they're going to succeed or recognize early enough before you've made a big investment that they're not going to succeed."

Data science can and should be an integral part of college and university operations. Institutional effectiveness should be working side-by-side with faculty and educators to collect, clean, and mine through data of current and past students' behaviors in order to better empower counseling and advisement services (whether virtual or otherwise). Data itself should be considered an asset to an institution, the data mining process a necessary function of institutional operations.

As for the ladder half of the Big Question, this book is a step-by-step practical application of old, new, and even experimental data science methods applied to higher education research. Instead of introducing terms and going through examples that have no meaning in the real world, this book uses real data and real examples to show you how real colleges and universities are making real changes —and all thanks to their newly found confidence in the analytics process.

It should be noted, however, that this book is not an in-depth field guide to any of the concepts presented. While I will be going to great lengths to explain some of the more commonly used methods, please consider any appearance of brevity on my part as an innocuous, latent encouragement to dive into other resources on your own. As with everything in the field of research, we must constantly consider ourselves students; as that old saying goes, "if there's one thing that I know it is that I know nothing." That being said, I will do what I can to fully flesh out the content that I feel is necessary in understanding the problems as much as possible within the confines of a single book.

INTENDED AUDIENCE

This book was intentionally written for science-minded educational researchers and scholar-practitioners, and anyone else concerned with predictive analytics in higher education. There are three main motivations that contributed to the late night and early morning keystrokes: first, it is my opinion that the overwhelming majority of data science text is unapproachable to decision-makers in higher education. Not everyone comes from a strong mathematics background, not everyone stays up to date with trends and current scientific literature, and not everyone is able to take the time to fully flesh out algorithms to the point that they can weight the pros and cons of using each of them.[1]

The second reason the audience of this book is higher education professionals is because there does not yet exist a large repository of predictive analytics examples in higher education. There are plenty of third-party vendors who supply predictive analytics, but when it comes to data science tutorials and walk-throughs specifically catered toward higher education, this book is indeed the first.

Finally, I want to write to higher education professionals because it is my belief that the tools I've developed and the research I've done in my career is not something to hold close to my chest. The best research is and has always been a collaborative effort, and it is my goal to bring powerful toolsets in computer science and statistics to the

---

[1]Well this is a little contradictory, isn't it? Are we supposed to stay abreast or are we supposed to read brief introductions to topics, like this book? Answer: *You must do both!*

higher education field in an approachable —and shareable —manner. By reading this book, I assume that you

- are an internal higher education stakeholder (i.e., anyone working in higher education or remotely associated with post-secondary education);

- are concerned about the decision-making process;

- know, at least to some degree, that the ability to understand institutional data is the key to surviving in tomorrow's educational landscape.

USING R FOR DATA SCIENCE

When I first started to write this book I knew I wanted to provide some practical application but I wasn't quite sure which direction I should take. I have performed data analysis in everything from C/C++ and Python to PHP and JavaScript, and with tools like Excel, Knime, RStudio, and a handful of others. As an intelligent person like you can understand, there are pros and cons of each system, and I had to weigh them out individually.

At the end of the day, I decided to use the R statistical programming language to do the practical applications in because it's just so darn easy to pick up and use no matter where you are on your path to statistical mastery. Have no experience with computer languages what-so-ever? You might feel a little overwhelmed at first, but you'll pick up on R pretty quickly. Mastered some other languages already? I honestly think you'll have the harder time adopting it because of some of its nuances, but you'll still be well ahead of the curve.

For the sake of your (and my) sanity, I've placed all the introductory R stuff at the back of the book. This allows us to focus on the data science concepts and gives you a special area in this book where we only talk about R. This section is more of a reference section; starting with multiple linear regression on page 77, I begin introducing R concepts as a way to help you discover statistics in R yourself.[2]

So what exactly is R and why are we using it? R is a statistical computing language that was developed by statisticians, which means that data analysis is a fundamental aspect of the language. This is, as you can probably already tell, a significant feature when compared to other general-purpose programming languages. While languages like Python are technically more powerful for larger projects, I've yet to find a language that allows me to intuitively prototype an idea and then explain that idea to someone else who is not a programmer by pointing to the code.[3]

Since a large portion of data science skills revolve around using machine learning to solve statistical problems, there will be progressively more and more R code as we dive into more complex topics. Focusing too much on the mathematics behind the methods is not the focus on this book. Instead, we will focus on the machine-learning aspects of data science, and in doing so, we will be using a lot of programming tools in R that let us take for granted the underlying statistical mathematics for a lot of things.

---

[2] If you really want a full-blown introduction to R and statistics at the same time, start with Andy Field's *Discovering Statistics Using R*. That book is still one that I reference daily when teaching both topics.

[3] You may have a different opinion about R, and that's fine. If you'd like to create examples in Python or C or JavaScript or even Brainfuck, go ahead and pass those along and I'd be happy to post them on this book's website.

WHY SHOULD ANYONE CARE ABOUT DATA SCIENCE?

If there's one thing the realm of education is ripe with, it's buzzwords. Data science isn't anything new; business intelligence and statistical inference has been around for a lot longer than you or I have, and slapping a new term on the task of mining through data to predict the future with some set degree of confidence is sure to turn off a lot of folks who have been around the block once or twice.

But data science is different from what you're used to. Instead of just taking some information from excel files, discretizing them, and then using something like stepwise binary regression to determine a possible trend, the field of Data Science concerns itself with taking *massive* amounts of data and finding a narrative within it. I like to use the following metaphor:

Think of every type of data that your institution collects as its own little book, and every piece of data a page in that book. If you were to take a whole library of all the data that your institution collects and rip out all the pages and throw them into a big pile, what would you get? (Probably a good rendition of your annual reports, but we won't go there!) Chaos, most likely. For many, many years, this pile of loose-leaf pages is all you've been working with because it's all you've known and it's all your systems can support, so the stories you read are just snapshots of bigger pictures. Sure, sometimes you'll get a page with some action on it, sometimes one with some good dialogue that will make you remember something else you've read some time ago, but you just can't quite remember how it's related...

Data Science is the art of carefully picking through that pile of book pages and putting together a complete book. It's the art of developing a narrative for your data, so that all the raw information that your institution warehouses and reports in bar charts and histographs is replaced with actionable intelligence.

HOW THIS BOOK IS WRITTEN

> *"No, no! The adventures first,"* said the Gryphon in
> an impatient tone: *"explanations take such a
> dreadful time."*
>
> –Lewis Carroll, *Alice in Wonderland*

When you picked this book up, you probably noticed that it doesn't quite feel like the other books that cover the same topics. One thing I noticed about all the texts available on applying statistics and computer science to social science data was that they were not very approachable by someone who wasn't already exposed to, say, an undergraduate curriculum in computer science or statistics. Talking with other people in higher education made me realize that for the vast majority of practitioners there is no real time nor desire to drudge through academic drivel and try to apply it to reality. This concern motivated me to take a more conversational approach to writing this book.

With that in mind, you can expect a lot of discussion in the pages ahead. Forget about handfuls of pages with formulas that just assume you are following the author along their rabbit hole of a journey into the depths of whatever they're trying to explain;[4] my focus is to engender dialogue and have a conversation with you. This means that you will

---

[4]That being said, there are a few moments when you have the option of learning more about a topic (like simple linear regression) but you can always skip the math-heavy pages if you're not interested.

have a lot more to read, yes, but it also means that (at least in my mind) the text is more approachable and easier to digest.

Now, you can't read a book about data science and ignore math entirely, but this is not a math heavy book *per se*; I will not go over crazy methods that involve some higher-level thinking, but I will use some math terminology and academic conventions in order to gently introduce you into some of the research that you'll no doubt start to seek out on your own. That being said, don't let anything you don't immediately understand be a turn-off. I try my best to create many footnotes with anything I can think of that might help expound on things that students have spent the most time with over the years, but there will always be concepts that will require further research on your part.

You can expect this book to focus on narrative case studies and storytelling, something that I have yet to see practiced in-depth among the literature that exists today. There is one exception: Andy Field's *Discovering Statistics using R*, but this book is very big and often intimidating for someone who only has time to read at night in bed when the kids are all asleep. I wrote this book thinking about scholar-practitioners in higher education and how they learn; I wrote this book to be more of a dialogue for someone who is interested in diving into their data and learning about it.

I want this book to be the springboard of your own personal data science learning journey. If we were to define a learning objective like good educators do, then I would say that the learning objective of this course is for you to begin asking the right questions about your data so that your institution can begin to explore it more efficiently.

1.1 WHAT YOU WILL (AND WILL NOT) FIND IN THIS BOOK

We're going to talk about basic machine learning and predictive analytics topics in this book. For subjects will be covered: simple linear regression, multiple regression, logistic regression, and Naive Bayes classification. These are all topics that have time and time again proved useful in higher education research.

I have purposefully omitted more advanced topics like K-nearest neighbor, decision trees, and support vector machines, because unless we are using massive data sets and unless we are trying to come up with a model that is enormously predictive,[5] we can rest assured that excellence in educational research will almost always begin with the basics.

---

[5]We're predicting human behavior most of the time, and humans are often difficult to predict. Models that are > 60% accurate in a given frame with a given set of data are often good enough to start informing smart decision that will, ultimately, benefit more students than a lack of effort will not.

Part I

Data Science and Education

Chapter 2

WHAT IS DATA SCIENCE?

> *"Intuition becomes increasingly valuable in the new*
> *information society precisely because there is so*
> *much data."*
>
> *–John Naisbitt*

Whether you majored in Computer Science and Statistics or Sociology and English (like I did), data science is about developing intuition. Practice, failure, and learning from failures creates within us an uncanny ability to see a new problem from angles that others may not be able to see, with implications that others may not be able to perceive, and to tackle that problem in a way that makes the most sense for our institution.

To define Data Science, we would have to first see where it sits among the other disciplines. Mathematics forms the foundation from which we can build algorithms and optimize numerical problems. Statistics give us the properties of those algorithms and the means with which to interpret them. Computer science gives us the means to analyze, optimize, and visualize those algorithms. Finally, Data Science is the combination of all three.[1]

There are many competing definitions of Data Science, but I will attempt to summarize the key arguments here. To start, you should know that the term "data science" has had a wishy-washy beginning in terms of definition, originally being a substitute for "computer science." As computers became more and more involved in the statistical analysis process throughout the latter third of the 20th century, it seems to me that people started to either stay on the traditional statistical path that relied heavily on mathematics or they diverged toward computational tools that did a lot of the math for them behind the scenes. Fast-forward to today and we have both sides of the house using computers and advanced algorithms to basically do the same thing: either *infer knowledge about the past* or *make predictions about the future*.

Wrapped up in all this is an apparent need to make statistics attractive. No one wants to just call themselves a statistician (myself included) because it's about as exciting as calling ourselves an accountant (sorry, accountants). Speaking of accounting, I remember in my graduate studies one student talking about entry level bookkeeping jobs and how boring they all sounded, until he stumbled across an opening for an "Entry-level Fiscal Data Analyst." The job description was no different than a general entry-level bookkeeper, but because he could call himself something other than bookkeeper (a term that

---

[1]Note that this is how *I* define Data Science, and your own mileage may vary. In fact, until we get a global consortium of data scientists and they all vote on a definition, we as scientists are bound to be blessed (cursed?) with multiple competing definitions, all coming from people who write books and think they know everything.

generally conjures up images of sitting in a cubicle and staring and spreadsheets while you wait until your lunch break to play Cones of Dunshire) he was excited to apply.

I see the same thing happening with statistics. In fact, as you go through this book you'll see a lot of stuff that looks just like statistics. And do you know why? *Because it is statistics, because that's what data science is.* Throughout this book I will use the standard industry buzzwords because that's why you picked up this book, isn't it? (Seriously, now. Would you have bought this book if it was called, "Introduction to Applied Statistical Pattern Recognition in Higher Education"? If you would then you're awesome. If not, well, I can't blame you.) This isn't to say that we can't use the buzzwords to help describe different aspects of the modern statistical process; all I'm trying to say is that you should focus more on honing your skills as a scientist and less on which buzzword you technically fall under.

To me, calling oneself a "data scientist" is a bit pompous. The best way I can explain why is through an analogy. When a programmer applies for a job, they don't just find a job opening for "computer programmer" and then apply to it; they will seek out a specific type of programming job that matches their unique skill set and then go from there. Some programmers deal purely with low-level machine code, like C or Java. Other programmers concern themselves only with web development, using tools like JavaScript, PHP, MySQL, and HTML/CSS. If I only knew JavaScript and called myself a computer programmer, I would technically not be lying —but I would also technically be misleading people.[2]

---

[2] In a similar vein, people calling themselves "data scientists" are rarely comprised of the vast eclectic skill sets that is commensurate with such a prominent title. Using a computer to solve statistical problems doesn't make you

Here are some buzzwords that I have heard people tell me should be included in this book: *Analytics, Predictive Analytics, Data Analytics, Business Analytics, Business Intelligence, Statistical Analytics, Data Science, Prescriptive Analytics,* and even *Analysis Science.*

If you are convinced that these are not buzzwords in higher education administration and that each one can have their own book written about them, I ask you this: how does defining separate roles within modern statistics help you do your job? At the end of the day, shouldn't we all be trying to sharpen our skills instead of polarizing our abilities under one descriptive roof?

What we try to accomplish with the professional application of science to datasets is bridge statistics and computer science in order to achieve one of two outcomes: make inferences about current and past relationships and/or information, and make predictions about future information. Data Science's focus is the synthesis of knowledge from data itself; I like to think that computer scientists branched off from math and statistics and started to be concerned mainly about prediction and accuracy rather than inference, and when data science gained popularity it did so because it brought back the "science" to the exploration of data.

It may be helpful to think of Data Science is a constantly evolving, constantly demanding discipline. You can't expect a complete crash course on the topic to be the last of it; the tools to carry out our analyses are constantly improving, and so we too must be constantly improving ourselves.

---

any more of a data scientist than me writing this book makes me a data scientist.

Chapter 3

THE DATA SCIENCE CYCLE

Data Science is comprised of five major components, each of which are covered in this book:

1. **Asking Data-Driven Questions** (in which you identify a target variable to predict or understand)

2. **Collecting and Preparing Data** (aka "Data Wrangling") (in which you identify features/potential predictors)

3. **Mining Data for Patterns** (aka "Data Mining") (in which you develop, test, and optimize models)

4. **Developing Knowledge** (dissemination, deployment, and sharing of both scholarly and non-scholarly workings)

Mastery of each component will not make you a "data scientist" *per se*, partly because there is no really formal, wholly accepted definition of what a data scientist is.[1] Just like anything else, the educational component can only take you so far; you must practice —and fail —many times before you can truly master something. Knowledge comes from education, but wisdom comes from experience.

3.1   ASKING DATA-DRIVEN QUESTIONS

At 7:30AM one day during a summer long forgotten, I was dragged into the Institutional Effectiveness Director's office and handed me a thumbdrive.

"I have an idea," he said. See if we can predict enrollments with all the student data on that thumbdrive.

Has this ever happened to you? It happens more often then not to me, and it's something that's easily avoided. If you don't see what's wrong here, it's that two researchers got together and tried to initiate a research project before *asking a research question.* Just like in any other scientific field, research begins by first identifying a topic and then drilling away the ambiguities until we arrive at a research question. If you think about it, you've probably met people who commit this scientific sin on a regular basis.

Starting a research project should always begin with a broad topic and slowly narrow down into a question that has obvious and measurable parts. For example, if I wanted to study enrollments and placement tests, I might develop a question like this:

1. How do placement test scores affect enrollments? *Too broad; What scores? What enrollments?*

---

[1]In fact, if you think about that term, it almost sounds redundant. It would be the equivalent of calling myself a Text Author instead of just Author.

2. What effects do placement test scores have on student enroll-ments? *Almost there; what effect?*

3. How do placement test scores influence what classes a student enrolls in?

Starting from the first bullet point and working down, I asked a broad question and then asked follow-up questions until I continued to restate my original question with more specificity. This process should not be new; developing a good research question is part of the freshmen college composition classes that I teach. However, many people often forget about specifying exactly what we will measure, which may lead to confusion or even lack of direction down the line.

This brings me to the most crucial part of research questions in data science. It's imperative that we are not only asking good research questions, but also that our questions are *data-driven* —that is, that we are conscious of a dataset somewhere that could be mined (or developed from scratch if need be) in order to measure the effect of a set of independent variables on a dependent variable. It makes no sense to wonder if we can predict some variable without at least hypothesizing about what variables might influence it. And do you know how you identify what variables may or may not influence your dependent variable?

(Cover your eyes!) A **literature review**.[2] That's right: you must identify a topic and then go read about that topic to identify gaps in research and literature that you can then attempt to fill in. If you find an area that has nothing written on it, great! You get to be the first

---

[2]Literature Review. n. 1. A summary of scholarly work around a specific topic. 2. A scientific requirement that is often neglected until after research is performed.

one. If you find an area that has a lot written on it, great! You probably don't have to waste your time researching something that's already been researched. The point is that as a scientific community, we owe it to each other to review *and contribute* to the existing body of literature pertaining to our topic.

Of course, nothing in this section should be new at all. *Do a literature review* and *ask data-driven questions* are things you should have been hearing about since day one. In my experience, however, higher education is more concerned with reporting data than they are about discovering relationships in data, and this creates an area where literature reviews are scoffed at and brushed off as a waste of time. To this I say reject the apathetic attitude toward scientific inquiry and embrace your scholarly roots.[3]

With a proper research question, we have the groundwork laid to begin collecting data for analysis.

3.2   COLLECTING AND PREPARING DATA

I remember the phone call very well. It was almost midnight, my kids were all asleep, and I had sneaked off to the kitchen table to get some

---

[3]The lack of a scientific community of inquiry in the community college environment where I worked frustrated me so much that in 2014 I created the Community College in Practice journal (ccjournal.org), an open-access, peer-reviewed repository of higher education research. My goal was to foster a Community of Practice for higher education scholar-practitioners, something that was not being done before. I always tell people that just because we work in higher education doesn't mean we are exempt from the nature of our profession; education has always been a social science, and we should be treating our work as such.

work done. My phone rang and I ignored it, but when it rang a second time I checked the number and saw that it was from Massachusetts. Knowing that an armless man could count on one hand how many people I knew from the Old Bay State, I figured it had to be something important and so I answered.

The person on the other end of the line identified themselves as a researcher from a university who happened to find my resume after mining through recommendations from colleagues. I was asked if I would like to help scaffold a new project that would involve mining through student loan data across about a dozen schools from all over the United States. My part would be to identify and plan out how the data would be aggregated and prepared for analysis. I of course accepted, then was in for a surprise when I got the specifications emailed to me.

This particular job stands out because it was one of my first exposures to higher education data warehousing[4] practices. Unfortunately, higher education was (and probably still is) a bit behind the times when it comes to information technology, and some of the things they were looking to do just didn't make much sense. For example, they wanted to have usernames and passwords to each of 12 colleges' database systems, and then wanted a researcher to login individually to each of the datasets to perform the same data pull 12 times (once for each college). This would create 12 separate reports on 12 separate templates (each college had their own unique reporting system), which now multiplies the time it takes to perform analysis by (you guessed it) 12.

The first thing I suggested was to get API access to these databases. If they were able to get that, we could create an interface that would

---

[4]We sometimes use the term *data warehousing* to describe the ways we are physically storing data.

translate an inputted query into 12 different API calls, then aggregate the responses so that we could get all of the results from each of the databases together in the same format. Since this was not possible,[5] I instead created a plan to develop our own relational database from all the other colleges' databases.

Whenever I'm trying to wrangle data from multiple databases that are in different formats, the first thing I remind people is that it's always easier to speak to three people in one language than it is to speak to three people in three languages. Each database was accessed and then a massive database dump file was created. We collected these double-digit gigabyte files and stuck them in the same folder, then started to build a custom database for our project so that each of the 12 colleges' data could coexist happily with each other.

Recall from the previous section that we should begin projects by *asking data-driven questions* (page 24). By doing this, we have both a clear direction for our analysis and a plan of attack for **data wrangling**.[6] In this particular case, the research team was looking to discover rela-

---

[5] I noticed that this was a recurring problem with the colleges I started to work with. The data warehousing systems they employed —which were usually third-party vendors who charged enormous annual fees —were often not capable of performing basic modern access techniques nor modern query and report design techniques. Most of the time you are forced to log in to a terribly outdated and poorly designed reporting interface and then stuck inside a software or web framework that is difficult to navigate and ends up breaking if you push it too hard.

[6] Data Wrangling is the process of "wrangling" data from multiple datasets in order to produce the most effective aggregate of raw inputs to work with. The idea actually goes as far back as the 80s. For example: *Discrimination and Classification* (Hand, 1981); *Discovering Casual Structure* (Glymour et al., 1987); *Algorithms for Clustering Data* (Jain & Dubes, 1988).

tionships between financial aid default and the types of classes that students took. Knowing this, we created a database with fields to account for the student's identification label (which we made up for security reasons), what classes the student took in the previous three years, the amount of financial aid they've been awarded, when the aid was awarded, and how often it's awarded, and the status of different services available to the student (like whether they participated in counseling, student services advising, etc). This new database structure served as our checklist for translating the information from the data dumps from each college into our new format.

We began to dig through the data dumps, and not just by transposing information from the colleges' data into our own database structure. After focusing in on one target variable (so we could then remove elements that obviously don't relate), new variables had to be made, old variables had to be omitted, and some data just had to be modified to account for hypotheses that we wanted to later test. Some examples include:

- Removing outliers with univariate analysis, residual analysis, etc.

- Discretizing variables or dichotomizing information so that it can be categorized

- Renaming, revaluing, transposing (e.g., stored data as [-1,1] changed to [0,1] because a negative value may interfere with the way we are mathematically validating our outcomes).

When it was all said and done, we had a database of financial aid and student enrollment information with which we could begin to mine for patterns and relationships. Interestingly —and frustratingly, especially the first time you experience this —the collection and prepa-ration of data will take up about 80-90% of the total project time. For this particular project I was working on, the actual mining portion took about a day, the validation a half a day, and then publication of the results about two hours. This is after spending over two weeks building the database!

You might hear this process called *data wrangling* (as I have called it), *data collection, knowledge discovery*, or something along those lines. However you refer to it, the process remains the same: aggregate data so we can start mining.

3.3   MINING DATA FOR PATTERNS

Early one morning I received a phone call from a distant community college research team asking me for a second opinion on a federal grant they were about to submit for funding. The project they were looking to fund was an exploratory data analysis effort to mine through a statewide public information system and detect patterns in data that could be published inside tools for use by higher education decision-makers. They were confident about the approach (especially because I had talked to them before about the possibility of publishing this type of research for all community colleges to benefit from) but they knew something was missing.

"To really hit this grant proposal out of the park," they told me, "we need a proof of concept." For that, they would need to generate a small-scale prototype of what the grant would be funding. Now, I know from experience (and you probably do, too) that mining through publicly-available higher education datasets published by a state entity is about as exciting and time-consuming as watching grass grow. On top of that, they needed to have a proof of concept before they submitted the grant proposal at the end of the week.

That college hired me to come up with a method and prototype for mining specific datasets and going through a knowledge discovery process.

In the 90's, Fayyad et al. (1996) used the term **Knowledge Discovery in Databases** (KDD) to explain the process of how aggregate data turns into information. Data is collected and then examined through a series of trials in order to come to a conclusive organizational plan with which experimental models will be tested. In a way, this process itself is experimental in nature because we are throwing broad-spectrum analysis techniques at our data and seeing if something sticks. Then, we continue the cleaning process from the previous step and further optimize our dataset so that whichever analytical tool we end up using is used properly.

When I arrived at the community college that hired me, they had already pulled down 10 years of public data from a statewide database published by their state's Community College Chancellor's Office. All of the information was in a single spreadsheet and they basically handed it to me and said, "What do we do?" I told them that being able to collect every single piece of information we can possibly think of may sound like a good idea, but irrelevant data will not help us form a narrative story[7] for our data. To determine which data we should be collecting, we often have to collect more than we anticipated and then perform

---

[7]When I teach analytics, I always point out that we should be looking at data like they are elements of a story. Some pieces are crucial to the narrative, while others can be left out and we would still get the same key points in the story.

a series of calculations to figure out which data fields to omit. From there we simply wash, rinse, and repeat.

The process of **data mining**[8] has three steps. First, we must identify what type of problem we are attempting to tackle by identifying a dependent variable. Generally speaking, there are two main types of problems in predictive analytics: *Regression* and *Classification*. When we want to fit a straight line through a set of data points that summaries a linear relationship between one or more variables, we are conducting **regression**. Alternatively, if we are trying to develop an algorithm that will correctly guess what label to give to a set of new data, then we are conducting **classification**. Both of these topics will be discussed at length in Part II of this book.

When I took a look at the data that the community college that hired me had, the first thing I noticed was that there was student outcomes data (grade distributions by student per class). Given this, I wondered if I could link any of the other data collected to the outcomes data in order to predict whether a student would pass a class given some criteria. By identifying my dependent variable —either pass or nopass —I also identified which type of problem I would be facing.[9]

After we've identified a variable that we wish to predict and the type of problem that we'll be tackling, the second step is to conduct analyses on the data to start building models. There are a number of

---

[8]Data mining —and any process where we go through data to look for patterns and relationships —is also called Exploratory Data Analysis (EDA).

[9]In this example, I realized that I was going to perform a classification problem as soon as I saw the variable I wanted to predict (which was the student outcomes variable). Sometimes you might go about this the opposite way; you may begin with the idea of wanting to predict a certain outcome and so you go to the data looking for a classification variable that fits the bill.

methodologies that could be used, including regression, classification, and clustering[10]. For the job that I was hired for, I decided to build a Naive Bayes Classifier —something we'll be doing together later in this book. Without going into too much detail, my algorithm basically looked at all the data in the dataset and built a bunch of rules based on patterns it found in trying to predict my target variable. The results of my exploratory analysis yielded a list of variables that were more important than the rest in predicting the value of my target variable, so I chunked my big dataset into smaller datasets that omitted the variables my algorithm said were not important.

The third final step in data mining is validation. You are probably familiar with statistical validation techniques, such as residuals analysis, test statistic analysis, and the like. For Machine Learning problems, these kinds of validation tools are often replaced with validation mechanisms that help to test a model's predictive accuracy. For the model that I developed, I used a popular technique called cross-validation.[11] Put simply, we split our subset data into, say, 10 different pieces, then we build a predictive model off of nine of those pieces and us the remaining one piece to test our model. This process is repeated 10 times so that each chunk of data gets a turn being the test set. We'll go into this technique in depth later in this book.

I chose to use a classification algorithm to create a decision tree that helped me to identify which variables we should be focusing on. The model's prototypical output was presented to the college that hired me and subsequently included in their grant application. Due to their

---

[10] Clustering is a type of classification problem, but here I have placed it alongside regression and classification because it's a powerful tool in exploratory data analysis.

[11] See page 140.

diligence and everyone's excitement over the possibilities that machine learning in higher education created, the grant was funded and they've been working on it ever since.

In summary, data mining requires that we:

1. **Identify** a target variable to predict

2. **Develop** models to predict the target variable

3. **Validate** the models to determine the most powerful one

Once we've developed a model and validated its efficacy, our next step is to deploy that model into the real world and start making a difference.

3.4   DEVELOPING KNOWLEDGE

Just like in regular ol' research, crunching numbers and coming up with inferences does no one any good if you hoard it all to yourself. We are all familiar with writing essays and reports, but these are just a small example of the ways we could be sharing and working with each others' work.

I am of the school of thought that the application of science to data is a communal one. Just like in any other scientific community, when we apply science to data and get it to tell a story, there are more than just consumers reading and using the information we've discovered. Our results and data should be published in such a way that it encourages other people to dive in and experiment themselves, perhaps even discovering improved methods of performing what we did and then subsequently sharing that with the community.

When we develop a predictive model, the research going into it (a literature review if your topic requires one, a methodology write-up, a step-by-step of what you did, and a follow-up discussion) is extremely important if anyone is going to replicate —or even understand, sometimes —your work. What's more important, though, is how your model is going to be used in real life. For this reason, the way you develop and disseminate knowledge is key to your model's place in the world of data knowledge.

I was once asked to speak at a web development conference hosted by a technical college, in which I was asked to go over how websites could connect users on the internet to complex database infrastructures full of information that companies wanted to make public but just didn't know how to. One of the things I introduced was the use of a web interface to run queries off of a cleaned and prepared dataset so that outside users could generate the same queries that researchers were using in generating their research results. This turned into a lengthy discussion afterwards with the keynote speaker about rethinking the way we disseminate research in the higher education community.

What we came up with was a general set of what one ought to do when developing knowledge, and came up with a phonetically similar acronym *AWT*. How AWT ("ought") we develop knowledge as higher education researchers? With *Articles*, *Websites*, and *Training*. For every data science project, there needs to be a common set of principles that exist for making your research accessible and available. This acronym outlines how a data science project could, at least at a minimum, develop knowledge.

- **Article**. The foundation of any data science project should be a research article. Whether you've written a lab report in the traditional *IMRAD* format or you've instead written an argumentative essay on the subject, there should be a body of literature for your project that clearly identifies where your project fits in the realm of things. I once received an email from a former student of mine telling me that her job would not allow her to write-up articles about the predictive models that they developed because they were bound by confidentiality agreements and publication of such classified results would lead to termination. I replied back that despite her employers resistance to share the results of scientific inquiry with the rest of the community, she should still seek to do what is scientifically right and perform a literature review before conducting an analysis. It's a shame that some knowledge is hidden behind patents and confidentiality agreements, but it is the nature of our world and the economic systems that run it. The best we can do is continue to do what is right in our hearts within the means provided and boundaries set before us.

- **Website**. It's New Year's Eve, 2014, as I sit and write this sentence. I just finished an online lecture recording where I discussed new age teaching methodologies (like video conferencing software and learning management systems that you can access from your phone) with a group of curriculum editors in New York. Last week, I was writing a JavaScript module to display a spreadsheet on a website in a way that non-technical users could edit it and download the data in a special PDF report template. Why am I mentioning all of this? Because we are past the days of journal-only research dissemination. Today, we've got websites, public code repositories, and more frameworks than you can shake a stick at. Don't limit yourself to a simple report to share your results.

- **Training**. Publishing the materials aren't enough, though. We must actively disseminate new knowledge and ideas among our communities so that other researchers engaged with their data have the most up-to-date skills and shared knowledge necessary to provide new interpretations and shared ideas to our data. We should be actively promoting the free, open distribution of research and learning materials, not hiding them behind paywalls or charging enormous conference fees where only a select few people are allowed to present.

We need to be thinking beyond the report, and concern ourselves with the importance of publishing our findings (and publishing what we didn't find), sharing our results via email, listservs, conferences, and other avenues of communication, and contributing to our own little community of practice. What are some other ways for scholar-practitioners like you and me to share and discuss our research?

Part II

Step-by-Step Machine Learning

Chapter 4

WHAT IS MACHINE LEARNING?

> *"We are drowning in information and starving for knowledge."*
>
> *–Rutherford D. Rogers*

In this book, we go over the two types of problems that we will face with our data: predicting numerical values and predicting class values. These are called *regression* and *classification* problems, respectively.[1]. If we focus on explaining relationships using regression or classification, we might call this process Statistics. If, however, we focus on predicting a numerical or classification value given new input, we might say we're doing **machine learning**.

Machine learning is nothing more than advanced statistics made possible with computers. However, statistics and machine learning have different desired outcomes: in statistics, we are looking to infer knowledge from relationships between variables; in machine learning,

---

[1]See page 32 for more.

we are generally looking to predict the values of some variables given the values of other variables. Is it possible to create predictions from statistics? Of course it is. Likewise, it is also possible to use machine learning to infer knowledge. The point here is that both fields are so uniquely intertwined that, like Sinatra once said, you can't have one without the other.

A basic understanding of statistics is necessary to appreciate what happens in machine learning. We'll see that throughout this book as we cover some concepts that you might feel are a bit novice. The reason we do this is because a lot of the statistical processes we've come to appreciate in our research are thrown out and replaced with overarching assumptions like the efficacy of a model given its performance during cross validation. Understanding and appreciating the underlying statistical methods behind what we're doing only enhances our ability to do predictive analytics.

If Machine Learning is nothing more than advanced statistics, why is it considered a different field? Well, there is a hidden joke in the worlds of data science, machine learning, and prediction computing that goes something like this: *everything boils down to statistics*. (I never said it was a good joke).

You see, when we talk about predicting a future variable based on a set of collected data, we are talking about the essence of what machine learning can do for us. Do we really care about the nature of the relationships between the predictors, the coefficients, or anything else? If all we are trying to do is predict some variable based on new input then probably not. However, if we peel back the layers of machine learning —creating a predictive model based off of a set of collected data that has a certain degree of predictive accuracy —then we can see how statistics forms the foundation of everything it is.

And that's the joke. When I started out with Machine Learning, what I was reading about was "regression optimization" and "density estimation." These things exist in machine learning, except they're called "supervised" and "unsupervised learning," respectively. In fact, you have probably already done a lot of machine learning without actually knowing it; the idea of "fitting" a model in statistics is part and parcel the idea of "learning" in machine learning.

Back to our original question. If Machine Learning is essentially just Statistics on steroids, why are they always considered two separate things? My take on this is that statistics has been around for a long time and computers have not. As such, the introduction of computer technology and the science of computing requires a new twist on an age-old concept. I think of it like two schools of psychological thought; mortality salience can technically be studied without touching Freud and Jung, but only in fully understanding and appreciating the underlying knowledge can a new psychologist attempt to make great strides in her or his research.

Perhaps one way to look at it is like this: if I give you a model, would you care about *why* certain variables predict some outcome even if having that knowledge will not change any predictive accuracy of this or any future models? Then dive right into Machine Learning and predict the future. If, however, you're attempting to explain a relationship between predictor and outcome variables in order to gain an understanding about said relationship, then you *must* master the underlying statistical knowledge that machine learning is based on.

For example, if I collected sector-specific stock market information and created a predictive model for day trading that boasts a 95% accuracy, do I really care about why the variables in the model are predictive? I do if I want to do research the right way; I don't if I'm only after a specific outcome (i.e., making money in the stock market).

You can do machine learning without statistics just like you can build a shed without studying carpentry. Just remember that what you get and what it's worth is a direct reflection of the sum total of what you put in.

Methodologically, the only real difference between the two is that machine learning emphasizes optimization and performance over inference. A machine-learning person and a statistics person, each describing the same model, would essentially focus on separate outcomes: the machine learning person would say "this model is 78% accurate in predicting x given a, b, and c," and the statistics person would say, "this model is 78% accurate in predicting x given a, b, and c, and I am 95% certain that you will achieve the same results."

So what gives, then? Why do you have people in one corner harping about p values and coefficients of determination, and then people in another corner talking about cross-validation and predictive accuracy? The answer is actually a really old one.[2]

Jerome Friedman wrote an article entitled, "Data Mining and Statistics: What's the Connection?", and in it he basically explained that most of these new buzzwords that data science and machine learning all sucked up probably would've been attributed to pure statistics had early statisticians not been so slow to the punch:

> One view says that our field should concentrate on that small part of information science that we do best, namely probabilistic inference based on mathematics. If this view is adopted, we should become resigned to the fact

---

[2]Okay, so it's less than twenty years old but more than ten years old. But hey, in computer years that's like, a whole century.

that the role of Statistics as a player in the "information revolution" will steadily diminish over time.

Another point of view holds that statistics ought to be concerned with data analysis. The field should be defined in terms of a set of *problems* —rather than a set of tools —that pertain to data. Should this point of view ever become the dominant one, a big change would be required in our practice and academic programs.

First and foremost, we would have to make peace with computing. It's here to stay; that's where the data is. This has been one of the most glaring omissions in the set of tools that have so far defined Statistics. Had we incorporated computing methodology from its inception as a fundamental statistical tool (as opposed to simply a convenient way to apply our existing tools) many of the other data related fields would not have needed to exist. They would have been part of our field.

What I think has happened over the years is that as computers became more and more easy to use and accessible to the layman researcher, new computational methodologies needed to be developed because those old farts in the stats courserooms couldn't possibly understand how to write shell scripts and code. Right? Right?

So we are left with a pretty embarrassing history of my profession and hobby. Everything I write about that concerns machine learning and data science is basically just statistics marketed as something else. Have I succumbed to buzzword hype and convinced myself that what I do is entirely separate of statistical influence? Of course not. But I do know this: every time I think I'm doing something amazing in machine learning, I can always find someone who did basically the same thing like 20 years ago in some old and long forgotten statistics journal article.

As we move forward in this book, let's consider that everything we do that involves statistical prediction is done so on a foundation of statistical knowledge. Statistics is indeed not so black and white as we often would like it to be; when a relationship is found between two variables with one criterion (like a p value) that same relationship could be scrutinized by looking at, say, the residuals. With machine learning, though, it's a bit more black and white; either one model outperforms another model or it does not, and each model is associated with some degree of predictive accuracy.

In the upcoming chapter, we'll get started with entry-level machine learning by predicting numerical values with regression. If this looks nothing like machine learning and more like statistics, that's because it is! The concepts, the way we think about our problem, and how we develop a solution, though, are all essential groundwork to understanding more advanced topics as we move forward.

Chapter 5

PREDICTING NUMERICAL VALUES WITH REGRESSION

Numerical prediction can be reduced to the simple concept of **regression**. Whenever we want to determine the formula for a straight line that can be drawn through the approximate "middle" of a set of plotted data, we are looking for a regression line. Regression equations are nothing more than the equation of a line, which looks a lot like $y = mx + b$. If you don't remember from high school, the m is called the slope and the b is called the intercept.

For our purposes, we don't use this slope formula exactly as is. Instead, we use **coefficients** to describe the relationship between the y variable and the x variable(s), so that in order to get the value of y_i, where i is the i-th element in our dataset, we multiply our predictor variable, or *feature*,[1] x_i by some coefficient β. Since each feature has its own coefficient, the individual effects of each feature variable on the

---

[1] These are also called "feature variables," as we will talk about later.

predicted outcome can be accounted for.

Regression is both simple and easy to implement, as evident by the fact that we are going to do everything by hand in the first section of this book (coming up next!). There will be a lot of math at first,[2] but most of it you can skip over if you just want to get right to the practical application.

So what does all this have to do with *Machine Learning*? A long time ago, after teaching an introductory class on machine learning, a student came up to me and asked why I only talked about regression. He told me that he learned about regression in his statistics class, and he thought that the machine learning class would teach him advanced statistical topics only. Unfortunately, this is a common mistake when it comes to understanding machine learning's relationship with statistics (and the reason why I wrote a whole section on it, starting on page 41).

5.1   SIMPLE LINEAR REGRESSION

There you are in your conference room. It's been about a month since Fall term started. Reports are due. Enrollment numbers are in. The screen turns on and up goes the slideshow with the barcharts and it's not good. Overall enrollments are up, but there's something odd with a specific course that your college has been offering. In DSC123, *Data Science for Higher Education*, more students are dropping out after the

---

[2] Remember that one of the essential parts of machine learning is that complex computer tools have been created in order to suppress the mathematical parts of the process from us. While I would never recommend skipping over gaining intuition about the mathematical foundations of what we learn in data science and machine learning, I would recommend diving in and gewhy tting results first in order to become properly motivated to proceed.

first census[3] than before. A certain someone (you know who) looks at you and says, "let's put together a report and see if we can get to the bottom of this."

Back in your office, you take a look at what you have available in front of you. There are spreadsheets of every type of student data one could possibly fathom all over your computer. There's the statewide management information system.[4] Then there's that spreadsheet you've been working on but haven't really been able to polish just yet. So what do you do?

"Duh!" you tell yourself. "I'll take a look at the courses and see what's changed." After mining through some SLO[5] reports, you determine that the department has changed their assessment procedures. Now, instead of having individual exams generated by each faculty member, two exhaustive tests are being given over the course of the course (of course): one just before census, and one just before the end of the course.

Being the savvy master of inference that you are, you hypothesize

---

[3] The "first census" is a measurement of enrollment activity for a college, often required by the state government as a means of counting enrollments based not on total class enrollments when a class starts, but rather, on the number of enrollments in that class after a specified amount of time has passed.

[4] Many states —counties, even —employ a management information system that districts can use to query state- and county-wide data repositories. You can probably spout off about ten of them off the top of your head, can't you?

[5] Student Learning Objective reports are generally due after each course is taught, and *should* give a broad overview of 1) what was taught, 2) how what was taught related to the SLOs, and 3) how (and why) the instructor chose the assessment method they did. If you're not having your faculty talk about both how and why students were assessed the way they were, it might be a good time to start!

that there is something about this first test that has altered student outcomes. Unfortunately, after talking with the faculty who designed this testing process, you discover that the exams are indeed legitimate and, while exhaustive, quite comprehensive. So you sit down with the faculty chair and devise a plan to start attacking drops in enrollment for this class.

"Students are dropping out after they fail the first exam," the faculty chair says. "We keep telling them they need to study harder for it than they're used to, but must students who've failed take that as, *oh, well, I'll just study for thirty minutes instead of fifteen.* They need to study longer than that, but I just don't know how long exactly."

The gears start moving in your head. The problem is that student outcomes have changed. The stimulus for this change is the new exam. The variable here is how long students need to study in order to get a good grade. If you could devise a model that correlates study time to exam scores, perhaps then the faculty could use this as a motivational tool for their students.[6] You tell the faculty member to email you all the data they have on study time and student outcomes on the exam, and that after some digging, you'll have a solution.

You head back to your office and remember this very story that you read in that one data science book for higher education. Being the professional data scientist that you are, you grab your copy of *Data Science in Higher Education* and flip open to this exact page.

---

[6] No matter how much time and energy we put into developing a model, it's up to the student to invest her or his time and energy to take advantage of the intervention opportunities that we develop or discover. You can lead a horse to water...

5.1.1   USING THE LEAST SQUARES METHOD

Let's get back to the basics with linear regression while we wait for that faculty chair to send us that email with all the outcomes data.

Linear regression is nothing more than taking a bunch of data and finding a straight line that fits the data as best as possible. "But any idiot can draw a line through data," you might say. And this is true: if you're given a plot of data with an obvious upward or downward trend, then sure, you can just draw a line through your data and slap it into a PowerPoint slide and be done with it.

If, however, you received your education from somewhere other than the London Institute of Applied Research,[7] you'll want your models to be as accurate as possible, and in order to do that we'll want to dive into some statistical mathematics.

Feshoop! There's your email from the faculty chair with the exam outcomes data.

Since we're concerned with the accuracy of our models, one of the things we'll account for in our math is *error*. Error in forecasting is calculated in many different ways and very differently from model to model, and for our purposes we'll be using a common method called the **Least Squares (LS)** method of linear regression model fitting.

The method of Least Squares fits a straight line through a set of n points in such a way that the vertical distances between the regression line points and the data points are as small as possible. In more specific terms, let D be the set of real data points and R be the set of points along the regression line. Least squares seeks to minimize the distance between $\{x_i, y_i\} \in R$ and $\{x_i, y_i\} \in D$.[8] We do this by finding the

---

[7]Hint: put together just the first letters.

[8]Put simply, our goal with least squares is to minimize the distance between

correlation between each point and correcting it with a ratio of standard deviations for these variables. In short, you get a line through your data that is as best of an estimate as possible of the middle.

So what does this line through our data actually *do*? A regression line fits our our data to a model (and the model fits the data with a regression line... it's all a happy statistical family!) and allows us to do two things: **project future values** of and **generalize information** about our data. This is made especially possible because the method we use to optimize the model, which is the least-squares method.

5.1.2 WHY DO WE USE LEAST SQUARES?

Skip this section if you couldn't care less about the theory behind using Least Squares versus other methods. We'll open up that email from the faculty chair and analyze the data starting on page 56.

You're still here? Great! If you've ever spent any time with plotting regression lines, you may have wondered why the least-squares method is so popular. I mean, why not just use the absolute error[9] and be done with it?

It turns out that least-squares is popular for two reasons. First, it is a relatively simple method compared to some of its counterparts (like

---

each point x, y on the regression line and each corresponding point from the actual data. Since our regression line is built off of a formula that we will generate, not all actual data points will be touched by the regression line. If we can somehow find a formula for a line that gets as close as possible to each data point, though, then we will have succeeded in performing a regression.

[9] Absolute error $|\epsilon| = |y - \hat{y}|$, where y is the actual value and $\hat{y}$ is the predicted value.

Least Absolute Deviation (LAD), in which we compare the absolute values of the literal differences between y and $\hat{y}$). Second —and probably more in line with a refutation of the LAD method —is that the least-squares method is more mathematically sound. Carl Gauss, a pretty important guy in the field of mathematics, showed that least-squares estimates happen to coincide with maximum-likelihood estimates when independent and normally distributed errors, a zero mean, and equal variances are assumed.[10]

Least-squares allows us to minimize the error by minimizing a quadratic function, something that is relatively easy if you remember that one class you took in high school. To minimize a quadratic function, you differentiate it and zero the derivatives, which leaves you with a linear equation —which is exactly what the regression **line** is!

To illustrate, let (y_i, x_i) be a series of data points for $i = 1, ..., n$, through which we will fit the following model:

$$y_i = ax_i + \varepsilon_i$$

where ε_i is the error of the approximation for the ith data point.

Now, watch what happens when we square and then sum the errors:

$$E = \sum_{i=1}^{n} \varepsilon_i^2 = \sum_{i=1}^{n} (y_i - ax_i)^2$$

Since our goal is to minimize the squared errors, we'll differentiate

---

[10] For history's sake, it should be noted that the least-squares method was first published in 1805 by a French mathematician who went by the name of Legendre. But to add scandal to the world of mathematical history (gasp!), Gauss published a paper in 1809 saying that he first used least-squares in 1795, which means *he* was its original creator. Dun dun dun!

and then set the derivative to zero (our optimum error):

$$\frac{\partial E}{\partial a} = -2 \sum_{i=1}^{n} x_i(y_i - ax_i) = 0$$

To understand why we use squares, we now rearrange the above formula to

$$\sum_{i=1}^{n} x_i y_i = a \sum_{i=1}^{n} x_i^2$$

which then gives us the least-squares estimate of the regression line (or slope):

$$a = \frac{\sum_{i=1}^{n} x_i y_i}{\sum_{i=1}^{n} x_i^2}$$

Squaring the errors rather than raising them to some other power results in a very manageable equation. If you have the time, go ahead and cube it and then email me to tell me how far you get before you see how much easier and approximate the least-squares method is. My email is jesse@lawsonry.com.

At the end of the day, regression tools like least-squares have two main purposes:

- **In regression analysis**, they can tell us how dependent the independent variable is on the dependent variable.

- In the calculation of a **correlation coefficient**, they can tell us about the interdependence of two variables that don't necessarily affect one another.[11]

---

[11] Regression is very similar to correlation. However, the two do not answer the same questions. Remember that correlation never implies causation

All this being said, there are some criticisms of least-squares, technically called ordinary least squares (OLS) when all the methods are in the same room. For example, Abdi (2007) points out that OLS estimates are the *best linear unbiased estimate*[12] when the following five rules are true: (1) the data is a true random sample of a well-defined population; (2) the population has a linear model; (3) the expected (ideal) error is zero; (4) the independent variables are linearly independent; (5) the homoscedasticity assumption is adhered to.[13]

Since the OLS is so heavily dependent on the homoscedasticity assumption, models developed for data coming from different subpopulations that contain independent estimations of error variance would be better served through the use of weighted least squares (WLS).[14] If, however, we're estimating parameters of a nonlinear function, the derivative approach won't necessarily work. Instead, we develop out iterative methods like Gradient Descent and Gauss-Newton approximations, both of which are advanced topics in machine learning reserved for a different book.

Alright, now let's get back to our problem!

—but that doesn't mean that two things cannot have both a correlative and causative relationship.

[12] These Gauss-Markov conditions can be remembered with the acronym "BLUE," and correspond to the theorem of the same name.

[13] According to Abdi (2007), the homoscedasticity assumption says that "the error is normally distributed and uncorrelated with the independent variables" (3).

[14] Also called generalized least squares (GLS).

5.1.3   ASKING DATA-DRIVEN QUESTIONS

At your desk, you open the email from the faculty chair and it says the following: "Here are the hours studies and final grade for the exam for five students."

Let X be the set that contains a list of hours studied for an exam and Y be the set that contains a list of scores on said exam.

We want to determine what sort of grade we can expect if we study for a certain amount of hours. This way, we can tell our students that if they study for t hours, they'll probably get a g grade. Like any good researcher, we'll start with our research question(s):

1. What is the expected grade given 0 hours of studying?

2. What is the expected grade given 2 hours of studying?

Now let's say we have a dataset of students that includes the number of hours they studied and their grade on a final exam:

Student #	Hours Studied (x)	Final Grade (y)
1	2	5
2	3	7
3	4	6
4	5	7
5	6	9

Table 5.1: Student outcomes data from the faculty chair about a new exam they've implemented.

For the purposes of our data, the final grade y is multiplied by 10 to give you the percentage grade (so a 5 would be 50%, 7 a 70%, etc).

To start making sense of all this, let's take a look at the linear regression equation:[15]

$$\hat{y} = \beta_0 + \beta_1 x$$

Here, $\hat{y}$ is the predicted value, β_0 is the y-intercept, and β_1 is the *slope*. Both β_0 & β_1 represent results of computations on cross products and squares that we'll need to account for in the next few pages. In doing so, we'll be accomplishing the central task of linear regression using the least-squares method, and that is **to minimize the sum of squared deviations**[16] (i.e., to minimize the distance of each observation to the regression line).

A note about symbols. For our purposes, we're using the greek letter beta (β) as a placeholder for the parameters of our function. It's important to understand only that the left of our equation is the function declaration and that the right part of our equation is our list of parameters, because as we dive into deeper and deeper topics like Machine Learning, we'll want start to adopt the verbiage traditional of such disciplines. Additionally, while we're using beta (β) in this chapter, future chapters will have similar linear equations that use different greek letters.

A little theory on regression. The theory behind linear regression is simple: using the data provided, we want to create a linear function that we can use to approximate forecasted values. In other words, we want to be able to draw a line through our data that is, at any point, as

---

[15] Said as, "y equals beta zero plus beta one plus the error", and the error is accounted for with the symbol *epsilon*.

[16] Sometimes this is called the *sum of squared errors*, or *sum of squares*. Generally speaking, when we talk about *deviation* or *error* we mean the same thing, but the least-squares method is different from other methods of error calculation, like *mean absolute error (MAE)* or *median error*.

close as possible to the surrounding data points, and we want to do this in such a way that if we were to draw that line out beyond our data we would get a reasonably accurate prediction of future data values.

Before we can calculate the sum of squared deviations, we'll do some simple math on our existing data. The first thing we'll do with our dataset is to expand it by two columns to create what's called a Sum of Squares and Cross-Product (SSCP) matrix. To answer our questions, we'll need to find the product of x and y as well as the sum of x^2. Let's expand out our table to do this:

#	x	y	Cross-Products (=xy)	Squares (=x^2)
1	2	5	19	4
2	3	7	21	9
3	4	6	24	16
4	5	7	35	25
5	6	9	54	36

Table 5.2: Outcomes data with SSCP matrix.

From here, we're going to calculate two different important variables.

The first thing we'll need is the **sum of the cross-product deviations**.[17] We use this to calculate β_1 from our linear regression formula (we'll get to β_1's formula in a bit). The second thing we'll need is the **sum of squared deviations**,[18] which is the other part of the equation

---

[17]Other popular names for this include *sum of cross deviations, sum of deviations,* and *sum of cross errors.*

[18]This can also be called the *sum of squares,* the *sum of squared error,* and *sum of squared pairs.*

for β_1.

Let c be the sum of cross product deviations, such that:

$$c = \sum_{i=1}^{n}(x_i - \bar{x})(y_i - \bar{y})$$

In essence, we're taking each x element and subtracting the mean of all x elements, then multiplying that by each y element that you subtract the mean of all y elements from. For our purposes, this can be simplified to the following:[19]

$$c = \sum_{i}(x_i y_i) - n\bar{x}\bar{y}$$

Much easier to read (and compute by hand!). Now we take the sum of the products of each x and y element and subtract from it the number of iterations n times the mean of x times the mean of y.

We'll use the values from our table to solve for c:

$$\begin{aligned}
c &= \sum_{i}(x_i y_i) - n\bar{x}\bar{y} \\
&= (10 + 21 + 24 + 35 + 54) - 5 \cdot 4 \cdot 6.8 \\
&= 144 - 136 \\
&= 8
\end{aligned}$$

Next, we need to get the sum of squared deviations. Let s be the sum of squared deviations such that:

$$s = \sum_{i=1}^{n}(x_i - \bar{x})^2$$

[19]What we've done here is simply distribute the n across the equation in order to make it more *paper-friendly* —that is, now we can do it on paper without writing out the means of x and y over and over again.

Thankfully, we can simplify this down some with a little bit of sigma simplification magic:

$$s = \sum_{i}^{n} x_i^2 - n(\bar{x})^2$$

From here, we'll compute the sum of squared deviations:

$$
\begin{aligned}
s &= \sum_{i}^{n} x_i^2 - n(\bar{x})^2 \\
  &= (4 + 9 + 16 + 25 + 36) - 5 \cdot 16 \\
  &= 90 - 80 \\
  &= 10
\end{aligned}
$$

Now that we have the **sum of cross-product deviations**, c, and the **sum of squares**, s, we can get back to our original regression formula and start solving for β:

$$\hat{y} = \beta_0 + \beta_1 x$$

With our sum of cross deviations and sum of squares, let's go ahead and compute the estimators β_0 and β_1.

β_1 is calculated by dividing the sum of cross deviations by the sum of squares, like this:

$$
\begin{aligned}
\beta_1 &= \frac{c}{s} \\
        &= 8/10 \\
        &= 0.8
\end{aligned}
$$

β_0 is calculated by subtracting the product of β_1 and $\bar{x}$ from $\bar{y}$, like this:

$$\beta_0 = \bar{y} - \beta_1 \bar{x}$$
$$= 6.8 - 0.8 \cdot 4$$
$$= 3.6$$

Now we have our original equation and all the parts that go in it. In the words of my old linear algebra teacher, "let's plug and chug!"

$$\hat{y} = \beta_0 + \beta_1 x$$
$$\hat{y} = 3.6 + 0.8x$$

And there you have it: your very own linear regression equation. You built that!

Let's take a look at what it looks like in graph form:

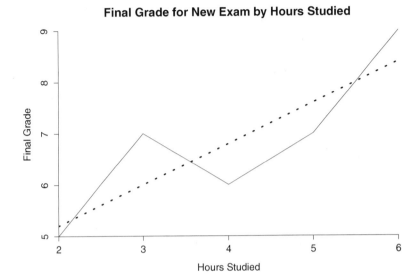

Final Grade for New Exam by Hours Studied

What I've done here is taken the data and plugged it into our linear equation. The dotted line represents the values of $\hat{y}$ as we inject the x values into the equation. Remember, the x values are nothing more than the amount of hours studying, and our linear function works by taking in the hours studied and pushing out the predicted final grade. Since the x axis represents our independent variable and our y axis represents our dependent variable, we can make some inferences based on this new, linear relationship that we've discovered.

WHAT CAN WE INFER?

- Since β_1 represents the change in y when x increases by one unit, we can infer that for every one hour of studying, a student's grade on the exam will increase by 8% (=0.8x10).

- A student who does not study at all can expect a final exam grade of 36% (3.6x10).

- A student who studies for 5 hours can expect a score of about 76% (jeez, this is a tough exam!).

That last point is illustrated with the following calculus: $\hat{y} = 3.6 + (0.8 \cdot 5) = 7.6$. Notice that in the table we have a student who did study for 5 hours and only received a 70%. Why the discrepancy?

This linear formula was developed taking into account the errors for the entire data set. The reason we use $\hat{y}$ and not y to represent what the regression function is plotting is because they're *estimates* and not definites.[20] One basic assumption of linear regression is that the true values of the data at each point along the regression line will be normally distributed.

5.1.4 PRACTICAL APPLICATION WITH R

Using R allows us to fast-forward through most of the math here by using the lm, or *linear model*, function.

Say we have a data1.csv file containing our data table of exam outcomes by hours studied, like this:

```
hours_studied,final_grade
2,5
3,7
```

---

[20] Don't make the assumption that all statistics texts will do the same, though. You'll often find formulas that use all sorts of symbols for different things. Remember that the concept of how to solve these problems is a lot more important than the symbology.

```
4,6
5,7
6,9
```

Notice that we only have the hours studied and the final grade. That's really all we need. For reference, this is the same information that was available in the first table back on page 56.

To load this into our project, we'd simply type:

```
> data1 <- read.csv("data1.csv")
```

Recall that in R we can access elements of our data by using the $ character after our data frame. For example, if we wanted to get values for the hours_studied column, we would simply type:

```
> data1$hours_studied
```

When you hit enter, you'll see the values for hours_studied:

```
[1] 2 3 4 5 6
```

That output basically says, "Here is the single-dimension vector result based on your request for all elements in the hours_studied column." Pretty neat, huh?

All of the math that we did in this chapter was based around finding two things: the **x-intercept**, which we called β_0, and the **slope**, which we called β_1. Using R, we can automatically compute the intercept and the slope by creating a linear model using the lm function. Simply type in:

```
> data1.lm <- lm(data1$final_grade ~ data1$hours_studied)
```

This basically tells R to describe `final_grade` by `hours_studied`, and do so by fitting a linear model. R knows to do this because of the tilde character, which, in `lm`, basically means "is to be described by." Thus, when you have `final_grade ~ hours_studied`, you are telling R that `final_grade` is to be described by `hours_studied`.

Behind the scenes, all the mathematical work is done for you. To get the intercept and slope that builds our linear equation, we'll simply query the coefficients element of our new data field `data1.lm`:

```
> data1.lm$coefficients
```

If you typed it in exactly like you see above, you should see a print out like this:

```
(Intercept) data1$hour_studied
     3.6                 0.8
```

This should speak for itself: you have the intercept, 3.6, and the slope indicated by the variable name `hours_studied`, 0.8. To turn this into a linear equation, you simply say that $\hat{y}$ is equal to the intercept plus the slope times x, or:

$$\hat{y} = yIntercept + slope \cdot x$$
$$= \beta_0 + \beta_1 x$$
$$= 3.6 + 0.8x$$

5.1.5 6-STEP SIMPLE LINEAR REGRESSION METHOD

Here are the steps necessary to complete a single variable linear regression model[21] Use this as a guide for the next problem that arises when you need to fit a simple linear function to a single-variable dataset:

1. Computer the Sum of Squares and Cross-Products (SSCP) by creating a SSCP matrix.

2. Find c, the sum of cross-product deviations (see page 59)

3. Find s, the sum of squared deviations (see page 59)

4. Find β_1, which equals $\frac{c}{s}$.

5. Find β_0, which equals $\bar{y} - \beta_1 \bar{x}$.

6. Plug and chug: $\hat{y} = \beta_0 + \beta_1 x$

There you have it: the 6-step linear regression method.

With your new formula, you can now confidently send an email back to the faculty chair and let her know about the new way to predict out student outcomes on that exam,[22] as well as share some of the insights you've discovered. After you send your email and start

---

[21]We might also call single-variable linear regression *simple* linear regression. It's called "single" variable because there is a single explanatory variable (the y variable) that is dependent on the incremental x variable.

[22]This is a good time to mention an important rule of data science (and machine learning, especially): any formula or model's efficacy is contingent on the limitations in scope of the data that was used to generate it. To put analogously, don't expect a model developed with 1990's data to be as effective with 2010's data.

thinking about where you'll get some lunch to celebrate your statistical accomplishment,[23] your phone rings.

"I saw the model you did for the faculty," a familiar voice says over the phone just as you realize that you should have left for lunch and waited for the inevitable email, "and we've gone ahead and developed three functions of our own. But we're stuck: We don't know how to find out which one is the best!"

5.1.6 LIMITED MODEL SELECTION WITH R-SQUARED

After discussing this request, you come to find out that whomever you're talking to really did follow all the steps on page 66 to develop a linear model. In fact, they did so well that when they got to scrubbing their data, they came up with three different models produced by three different people. Naturally, they'll want to create some predictions and then test those predictions in order to determine which function might be the best fit given their data. Comparing multiple functions to determine which one is the best fit is referred to as *model selection*.

"How can there be multiple functions?" someone in your office asks. After you glare at them for a second (don't you hate when people read your screen over their shoulders?) you clear your throat and explain what's happening, reciting what you remember on page 67:

Whenever we're working with regression problems, we're dealing with all sorts of numerical data types. Sometimes those numbers represent actual values of whatever they've measured, like the case of a discrete variable indicating the number of xs that have done some-

---

[23] Hey, in the world of unknowns that we live in every day, we have to take our victories one at a time. If you made it with me this far, go get yourself something tasty to eat or drink. You deserve it!

thing; other times those numbers represent associated or related values because we may a) enumerate a numerical dataset in order to make its ranges of values more manageable, b) round up or down when dealing with fractions of numbers, or c) change the numbers based on some external data scrubbing rule that we created somewhere.

Since there are all kinds of different things we can do to numbers in a dataset, what many data scientists like yourself often do is create multiple functions to create multiple predictions.

For example, let's think back to the student exam outcomes data table on page 56. One of the assumptions we make from the data is that the numerical value for hours_studied represents an estimated studytime. Since this is probably a self-reported metric and it's doubtful that any fraction of time spent studying was accounted for,[24] we might duplicate this dataset and then modify the study times based on what the students actually reported. So, if we look at our survey results and find things like, "I studied for a little over an hour," or, "I studied for about two hours," we can modify the hours_studied feature in our duplicated dataset to reflect this.

Now we have two datasets that will produce two different linear functions. The first original dataset will produce the function we created in the last chapter, and our new dataset containing estimated intervals of 15 minutes for each dataset (based on whatever was reported in the hypothetical survey results we've been discussing) produces an entirely new linear function.[25]

---

[24] I don't know any students who would say, "I studied for approximately 3.47 hours and achieved a 79.44% on my exam." If you know of any university producing students like that, then please send me an email.

[25] At this point I just want to remind you that we're talking about a hypothetical second data set that we built in conjunction with our first data set about

Feshoop! The dreaded email. You open it up and its the followup to the phone conversation you just had. In it, there is a desperate plea for help:

"We have five functions that are plotting a regression of grade outcomes given a final exam score, each from one of five different faculty members. Can you help us determine which one should be employed going into next year?"

Here are the functions they came up with:

$$\#1 : \hat{y} = 3.6 + 0.70x$$
$$\#2 : \hat{y} = 3.6 + 0.75x$$
$$\#3 : \hat{y} = 3.6 + 0.80x$$
$$\#4 : \hat{y} = 3.6 + 0.85x$$
$$\#5 : \hat{y} = 3.6 + 0.90x$$

For simplicity's sake, these people are using the *exact same dataset* as before; these functions represent the predicted grade on a final exam ($\hat{y}$) given the independent variable hours_studied (x). Let's forget for a moment that if they had followed the the steps in this chapter they wouldn't have come up with competing models because the ordinary least squares calculations would have given them one model. Nevertheless, the purpose of this section is two-fold:

First, we should always expect to work with competing models. It would be pointless for us to only use one method to predict some value or outcome and not allow other methods to compete for exposure. In data science, we practitioners should be less in love with the different methods that we're comfortable with and more in love with finding the most efficient method to solve our problem. Most of that time that

---

the student outcomes from the exam back on page 56.

means that we're hitting the books and learning (or re-learning) some obscure mathematical concept in order to present it. By presenting multiple possible outcomes of a group of models, we can begin to reduce our uncertainty about a certain group of predictions.

Let's look at this another way. Whenever you develop a model with the intention to make a prediction, you'll want to first take steps to reduce the level of model deployment uncertainty present. Uncertainty in predictive analytics generally takes the form of a negative confidence level associated with the deployment of a predictive model. That is, you'll be more uncertain (unconfident) about the results of a model unless steps are taken to reduce that uncertainty. The most practical method of reducing this uncertainty is through cross-validation. might consider the development and subsequent comparison of multiple models a method of cross-validation. The results of this effort will only strengthen your confidence in supporting the prediction model that you champion.

Whenever you're comparing functions, it's good to frame the activity within the context of data science; developing "models" —a fancy word for *functions*[26] —from data is known as "training" a model, and making predictions (and measuring how accurate those predictions are) is known as "testing" a model. In our example three functions, the faculty that developed these models have already completed the first part (the training). It is now up to us to test the models in order to select the best one to use.

---

[26] In this book and any other book on data science, you will often see the terms *model* and *function* used interchangeably.

5.1.7   THE PROS AND CONS OF R-SQUARED

As the statistician George Box once said, "All models are wrong, but some are useful." Nothing is ever certain in data science unless you happen to be studying how execreble Vogon poetry is to the human ear. Our goal when creating models to make predictions is to reduce the level of uncertainty (also called *inverse confidence*) surrounding the deployment of a particular model from a set of models for a given problem. Increasing our confidence in a model is known as measuring for *goodness of fit*, or *model selection*.

Since we're dealing with a handful of simple linear functions that all contain the same number of parameters and try to solve the exact same problem, we can use a popular model selection method called *R squared*. R-squared measures how well a regression line fits a given dataset, and in this way, tells us about the variation of outcomes explained by the model by giving us a percentage of explained variability. It's value is roughly interpreted as follows: as r-squared approaches zero, the model explains less of the variability of the response data around its mean; as r-squared approaches 1, the model explains more of the variability of the reponse data around its mean. An r-squared of 1 indicates that a model explains 100% of the variability in the response data. In other words, when $r^2 = 1$ you have a regression line that fits the data perfectly.

Why do we use it? It's a popular method for two reasons: first, it's mathematically logical in that calculating it requires (simple) manipulation of existing data on-hand. The formula for R^2 is the residual sum of squares divided by :

$$R^2 = \frac{\sum_i^n (\hat{y}_i - \bar{y})^2}{\sum_i^n (y_i - \bar{y})^2}$$

As you can see, all you need to calculate this is your model's predictions ($\hat{y}$), your model's dependent variable (y), and the mean of your dependent variables ($\bar{y}$).

The second reason R^2 is so popular is because of what I call the Celebrity Effect; since everyone is so used to seeing the darn thing, it makes sense that everyone would want to implement it. This isn't to say that it's the wrong choice for model selection at all. In fact, it's quite useful for quickly selecting the most efficient of a set of simple linear models.

that being said, there are problems with using r-squared that are often overlooked among practitioners. Perhaps the most prevalent issue is that people think you have to shoot for the highest r-squared value as possible. In theory this makes sense —a higher r-squared value indicates a higher degree of explaining the variance in response data —but the latent effect of this line of thinking is that *any* predictor that increases r-squared is technically considered significant (because we're defining significance based on r-squared influence).

Let's consider an example. Say we are pondering over our final exam results table and discover that we can create a new column called did_study, which takes a binary value [0,1], 0 if the student did not study, and 1 if the student did study. Since each value of 1 will correspond to a variable result, we end up with a higher r-squared than before purely because we have this *proxy variable* that doesn't really help to explain our data anymore than our previous model did with that new variable excluded. If you chased r-squared, though, you would see that it was a significant predictor (when in reality it wasn't).[27]

Another problem with r-squared is that it does not predict the efficacy or predictive capabilities of a model. You can have a great model with a small R^2 and you can have a terrible model with a high R^2. You should never use this metric as a way to advertise a model's performance because it doesn't mean anything outside the context of its fellow models for the same dataset. If you show me one model and then tell me its r-squared value, I'll immediately ask to see the values of its sister models. While this is not industry-standard practice, I encourage you to keep in mind the following: *an r-squared score alone doesn't tell me anything!*

In summary, R^2 a) indicates that some percentage of the variation in the dependent variable can be explained by its relationship to the independent variable, b) *cannot* determine whether estimates and predictions are biased, and c) *does not* indicate whether a regression model is accurate or not.

Even so, it's a) widely used among many different fields in limited model selection, b) is easy to calculate, and c) helps to convey your model to other practitioners.

I'd also like to note that there are certain disciplines in which you should expect a low R^2 —that is, certain fields produce models that will not be as effective in explaining the variation in the dependent

---

[27] Analysts typically think of r-squared as similarity, when in fact you could have a very high (greater than, say, 90%) r-squared with an even higher negative correlation! If you consider a scissor chart —when you have one line that increases from bottom to top and another line that decreases from top to bottom —then you would note that a high r-squared certainly does not indicate a causal relationship (because the values are completely opposite of one another!).

variable because of the human factor. The fact of the matter is this: when trying to predict human behavior, no model will ever be entirely accurate. It goes without saying then that you should expect low R^2 scores (circa 25%, give or take) when dealing with human behavior.

BUILDING A TABLE TO COMPARE R-SQUARED

When you have several models that you want to compare, each containing the same amount of parameters and each developed from the same dataset, you can quickly select the most efficient model by calculating each of their R^2 values and choosing the model with the highest. To do this, you must first create a set of predictions ($\hat{y}$) for each of your models. Then, you use those predictions to calculate the residual sum of squares. Finally, you divide each model's residual sum of squares by the total sum of squares to get their r-squared values.

If you recall from page 69, we have a total of five functions to choose from. Our job will be to apply these functions to the data from the table on page 58, but we only need to worry about the independent variable x and the resultant final grade y. With these, we'll be able to plug in x_i to each of our linear functions, produce a predicted value for the final exam ($\hat{y}$), and then calculate our R^2.

To do this, we'll create a new set of tables (one for each function) with the $\hat{y}$ and residual sum of squares for each model in each respective table. The first column is created by simply plugging in the x value from the dataset into each function and then documenting the resultant $\hat{y}$. The second column is calculated by using the formula for the residual sum of squares, which is the squared difference between the actual value (y) and the predicted value ($\hat{y}$) such that $RSS = \sum_i^n (y_i - \hat{y}_i)^2$.

You can see in table 5.3 that we've pulled in the #, hours_studied, and final_grade features[28] from the table on page 56 to help build the columns for #, the independent variable (x), and the dependent variable ($\hat{y}$), respectively. To reiterate, the $\hat{y}$ is calculated by taking the values from the x rows and plugging them into the first function from the list on page 69. The RS —the "residual square" —is then calculated by squaring the difference between the actual value and the predicted value (see Table 5.3).

#	x	y	$\hat{y}$	RS	TS
1	2	5	5.0	0.00	3.24
2	3	7	5.7	1.69	0.04
3	4	6	6.4	0.16	0.64
4	5	7	7.1	0.01	0.04
5	6	9	7.8	1.44	4.84

Table 5.3: R-squared table for Model 1 (M_1), which is the linear function $\hat{y} = 3.6 + 0.70x$

From there, we'll do the same thing for each of the other four functions and plug them into their own set of columns in our table (Table 5.4).

Recall that the RS field is just the residual square; we still have to get the residual *sum* of squares, and we do that by adding together

[28]This is the first time we've talked about predictors being called "features," but it wont be the last. In Machine Learning applications, you'll often hear the variables used to populate a model's parameters being classified by the name of their set, which we call a *feature* of the data.

M1		**M2**		**M3**		**M4**		**M5**	
$\hat{y}$	RS	$\hat{y}$	RS	$\hat{y}$	RS	$\hat{y}$	RS	$\hat{y}$	RS
5.00	0.00	5.10	0.01	5.20	0.04	5.30	0.09	5.40	0.16
5.70	1.69	5.85	1.32	6.00	1.00	6.15	0.72	6.30	0.49
6.40	0.16	6.60	0.36	6.80	0.64	7.00	1.00	7.40	1.44
7.10	0.01	7.35	0.12	7.60	0.60	7.85	0.72	8.10	1.21
7.80	1.44	8.10	0.81	8.40	0.36	8.70	0.09	9.00	0.00
RSS:	3.30	RSS:	2.63	RSS:	2.40	RSS:	2.62	RSS:	3.3
TSS:	8.80	TSS:	8.80	TSS:	8.80	TSS:	8.80	TSS:	8.80
R^2	**.625**	R^2	**.702**	R^2	**.727**	R^2	**.702**	R^2	**.625**

Table 5.4: R-squared table for Models M_1-M_5

all the elements of the RS column. Also recall that the Total Sum of Squares (TSS) is going to be the same for all models, because $TSS = \sum(y_i - \bar{y})^2$), and neither y nor $\bar{y}$ changes when we go from model to model. To calculate R^2 for each model, then, we take the RSS for each model (which I've already calculated at the bottom of each model's columns in table 5.4) and divide it by TSS, which, for this dataset, was found to be 8.8.[29]

Which model do we choose? Choosing the best model is easier than you think, unless you already think that we just choose the model with the highest R^2 —because that's exactly what we do. The model with the highest R^2 —or, put another way, *the model that explains the most variance in the data* —is the third model, which just so happens to

---

[29]I calculated the Total Sum of Squares by adding up all the elements in the Total Squares (TS) column of table 5.3. Since TSS is calculating by squaring the difference between y and $\bar{y}$, TSS will be the same for every model.

be the one that we developed by hand using the sum of squares and cross-products matrix back on page 58.

Our goal in this section was the select the most appropriate model from a list of five that a faculty chair sent to us. Given the results of our R^2 table, we can write back to the faculty member that the third model should be selected because it explains the most variance in the data. Go get yourself a coffee (unless you're reading this at night, then maybe some water) because you've done a great job following along!

5.2 MULTIPLE LINEAR REGRESSION

Up until this point we have been doing everything by hand. What I mean by that is that we have extrapolated every mathematical necessity from the simple linear regression methodology and gone through each equation one by one. As I will consistently reiterate throughout this book, one of the fundamental niceties of machine learning is that we don't have to worry about some of the nitty-gritty behind-the-scenes math because we have tools that do it automatically.[30] For this next section on multiple linear regression, we'll concern ourselves less with the math and more with the process.

Starting from here, we will be using R to help explain a lot of things. If you haven't set it up yet, now is the time!

Feshoop! Another email. It's great how in this fictional narrative there are never any days off, isn't it? You open it and it's a plea for help

---

[30]We are still going to go over the math, though, because I think exposure to how an engine works will make you a more capable motor vehicle operator.

from the Student Success Center: *We need to submit our program budget for next year and we need to cut one of our programs. Which one has the least amount of influence on student success?* After coming to the realization that you definitely need another researcher in your office, you agree to help and ask for more information.

5.2.1   ASKING DATA-DRIVEN QUESTIONS

In the previous section we were trying to explain a student's test score as a function of hours studied. Using one variable to explain another variable lends itself to simplicity but also to the largest fallacy of descriptive statistics. I'm reminded of a quote from the late Andrejs Dunkels that I'll butcher up: statistics make it easy to lie and hard to tell the truth.

As practitioners, it's our job to ensure that however we're describing our variable's relationship(s) to (an)other variable(s), the explanation is the best fit for the data in question. In this way, our job is similar to how we approach optimization in mathematics: we want to optimize our formulas as much as possible. While some variables really can be explained entirely by another variable,[31] often times there will be many different factors involved in explaining some variable instead of just one.

A *multiple linear regression* is nothing more than a regression that has two or more explanatory variables. Just like with simple linear regression, our resultant product is a single straight line with which we can predict future values of our target variable. In this section, our

---

[31]If this is the case we could probably say that there is *causality*, which is something that a lot of people want to do but are not able given the nature of their experiments.

target variable will be the English placement test scores given the final class score for five pre-placement test classes provided by the Student Success Center. Since we're using R to do this, *we're going to complete all the math involved with one simple command.* But first, let's flesh out what we're dealing with.

The coordinator already provided us with a research question, which we might state as follows:

What is the relationship between our pilot pre-placement test writing classes and placement test scores?

We want to do two things: First, we want to compare the means of the two groups in order to report whether a difference exists (because this will be the easiest thing); second, we want to determine whether a predictive model can be created in order to help market the efficacy of the pre-placement test writing classes.

Since the coordinator already has a hypothesis in mind—and since we want to start our project by asking data-driven questions—let's go ahead and use that as our hypothesis going forward in comparing the means of the two groups:

$H1_a$: *Students who take pre-placement writing classes have a significantly higher average score ($p < 0.05$) on the English placement test than those who do not take the test.*

$H1_0$: *Students who take pre-placement writing classes do not have a significantly higher average score ($p > 0.05$) on the English placement test than those who do not take the test.*

You'll notice here that we're using a *one-tailed hypothesis*, which means that we're testing for a change in one direction of the mean of each group. When testing for the effect of some independent variable on the outcome of exam scores, I would usually recommend using a two-tailed test because it allows you to measure whether the experimental group's mean[32] is greater *or* less than the control group's mean,[33] but because I want to provide as much diagnostic power as possible to testing whether there is only a positive result (i.e., I don't really care to test whether the result of the writing classes has a negative effect on placement test scores because that idea does not align with my hypothesis), I will opt for a one-tailed hypothesis that seeks an effect in one direction.

Why choose a one-tailed hypothesis? The benefit of using a one-tailed hypothesis is that I am saving myself some analytical work in the future by marrying up my hypothesis (that the classes increase placement test scores) with my expected result. Since I am expecting pre-placement test writing classes to increase a student's score on an English placement test, my one-tailed hypothesis gives me an alpha of 5% ($\alpha = 0.05$), which means that a difference in means will be considered significant if the test statistic is within the top 5% of the probability distribution.

Could we use a two-tailed hypothesis? Technically we could alter our hypothesis to determine whether there is any difference in means, but I'm not interested in whether there is a negative effect. One argument for doing a two-tailed test, however, might be that it would be unethical to taxpayers to have a program that did not result in a significant improvement in student outcomes (if that is indeed the intended effect of the program). A two-tailed test might help to determine whether the pre-writing classes are either helping or not helping

---

[32]The experimental group in this case would be the group of students that did take the pre-placement writing courses.

[33]The control group would be the students who did not take any pre-placement writing courses.

students, but I am injecting some professional judgment by opting not
to test both directions for two reasons:

- I know from experience in researching and writing about the
  topic that pre-placement test preparation results in higher placement test scores, and there's nothing wrong with formulating a
  hypothesis based on my own personal prior knowledge (that's
  why they're called hypotheses);

- a two-tailed test forces us to split the alpha value in half, meaning that significance will only be achieved if the test statistic
  is within the top or bottom 2.5% of the probability distribution.
  Since I am more concerned with whether there is a significantly
  higher ($p < 0.05$) average score than I am concerned about
  whether exam scores are extremely different ($p > 0.025, p <
  0.025$), the one-tailed test seems more appropriate.[34]

---

[34] Ethics should come into play when determining whether a one-tailed test
is appropriate. For example, you should never choose a one-tailed test for
the sole purpose of achieving significance. Deriving a one-tailed test from
a failed two-tailed test is unethical and leads to misinformation. Another
example of when a one-tailed test is not appropriate is when there are con-
sequences of missing an effect in the other direction. In medical research,
for example, a one-tailed test of whether a new drug helps people feel less
depressed has the latent consequence of not testing whether the drug makes
people feel *more* depressed by not testing the opposite direction. If I was
not confident of the prior research involved in pre-placement test courses
and their effects on placement test scores —or if we were exploring a field
that was still immature —then I would definitely opt to use a two-tailed test
because it would be unethical to fund a program that had negative student
outcome results. Consider these ideas when formulating your hypotheses
and thinking about your research in the future.

5.2.2 COLLECTING AND PREPARING DATA

Here's some back-story:

One year ago your college decided to run a pilot program at the Student Success Center (SSC). The program offered students a set of five writing classes (that all had to be taken together) that could be completed before taking the English placement test.[35]

After contacting Doug, the SSC Coordinator, he explains the data that they've been collecting (and that he'll forward to you):

> Thank you so much for helping us out. We have been running a pilot program of five writing classes that are designed to help students get higher scores on the English placement test. Next year, we will only have money to fund four classes so we will have to drop one if you determine that the program is indeed effective.

> We have data on 72 students, each of whom have taken all five courses and then taken the placement test. Currently, the average placement test score for students who do not take our pre-placement test writing classes is 82.63%. We believe that students who take our courses will outperform students who do not.

> I need two things:

> 1. I need to know which class has the least effect on the

---

[35] Most colleges require first-time students to complete placements tests for Math and English in order to get them into an appropriately rigorous general education track. The scores you get on the placement tests will determine which level of classes you will be enrolled in —and also may limit your future major opportunities.

student's placement test score so that it can be dropped from the curriculum.

2. I would also like to be able to explain to the budget committee that participating in our pre-placement test classes will have a positive effect on English placement test scores.

Thanks!

To get started with this study, we'll first need to acquire the data. In the fictitious world that exists inside this book, Doug the Coordinator has already emailed you the CSV file containing the data he's collected and I've long since retired somewhere in northern Maine to live out my dream of writing all day in a cabin in the woods. In real life, you can download the two CSV files for this section from this book's website.[36] Go ahead and do that now.

By this point you should have an R environment setup and running on your computer. If you have neglected R up to this point then you're part of the problem in this world and you should put this book down and sit in the corner of your house for at least fifteen minutes thinking about your failure. (Hey, lighten up!). When you're done, go to your favorite search engine and look up a tutorial for getting setup with R on your specific operating system. You don't have to dive too far into R just yet, but you will want to have a general understanding of the syntax and concepts.

---

[36] Go to lawsonry.com/datasciencebook and click on the "Datasets" link in the navigation menu. Scroll down until you find the datasets entitled "pre-placement scores with classes (CSV)" and "pre-placement scores without classes (CSV)"

Once you've obtained the data file, put it in a new project directory and open up your R environment (which is probably RStudio). Now we're ready to get started!

The first thing we'll do is read the CSV file without our pre-placement test classes into R. We do this pretty easily:

```
> withoutclasses <- read.csv("preplacement-scores-without-classes.csv")
```

This will cause R to create a new **dataframe**, which is a type of in-memory way that R stores data, called withoutclasses. I always think of a dataframe as being a simple spreadsheet. In fact, if you're using RStudio, when you preview the dataframe it will look like a mini spreadsheet. This is a neat way to think about using R because most of us are already familiar with Excel anyway.

The read.csv command created a new variable withoutclasses and used R's wonky[37] assignment operator <- to assign the contents of the CSV file to it.

Now our CSV is in memory. We can verify this by dumping the entire contents of our withoutclasses variable into the R terminal by typing in the variable's name and hitting enter. Try it!

```
> withoutclasses
```

You'll see all 72 entries outputted into the console. For simplicity's sake, here's just the first few lines from when I entered the above

---

[37] R uses a left arrow looking thing (<-) for assigning values, and this is probably due to the fact that the traditional assignment operator (=) is not technically correct. When we assign values we are not saying that something equals something else, only that something *represents* something else. There are plenty of nerd debates you can look into if you're passionate about this. I am not.

command:[38]

```
  student score
1       1    78
2       2    75
3       3    85
4       4    82
5       5    82
6       6    85
...
```

Next, we'll go ahead and read in the CSV containing data from students who did take the pre-placement test classes. Let's read them into a new variable called withclasses, then verify its contents:

```
> withclasses <- read.csv("preplacement-scores-with-classes.csv")
> withclasses
```

```
  student class_1 class_2 class_3 class_4 class_5 score
1       1      99      99      94      82      78    97
2       2      81      92      82      95      79    91
3       3      97      81      78      86      76    87
4       4      94      97      94      97      77    96
5       5      84     100     100      86      80    98
6       6      80      99      93      80      79    95
...
```

---

[38]You can get the head of your dataset —that is, the first handful of rows —by using the function head(). To get the results I got here, simply type in head(withoutclasses).

Taking a look at our dataframe in RStudio you can see that the left column is the student number, columns two through six indicate the score a student earned in each of the five pre-placement test classes, and the last column on the right is the student's placement test score on the English section. Remember: we're looking to determine 1) which class is least effective, and 2) the average score for students who take these pre-placement test classes (so that we can compare it to the average score of students who do not take these classes).

For that second part, a simple comparison of means via t-test is all we need. For the first part, though, we'll get down and dirty with some linear models.

5.2.3   MINING DATA FOR PATTERNS

Let's cover some math concepts really quick and then jump right into the R code. **All of this complex math will be carried out behind the scenes in a single line of code**, so don't go anywhere just yet!

Recall from the simple linear regression chapter before this one that our task from here is to complete a bunch of math in order to calculate the coefficients for a regression equation. If the simple linear regression line formula is

$$\hat{y} = \beta_0 + \beta_1 x$$

then the multiple regression line formula is simply

$$\hat{y} = \beta_0 + \beta_1 x_1 + \dots + \beta_i x_i$$

The only thing that's different is that now we have a variable amount of coefficients and independent variables. For our pre-placement test problem we are working through, we have five different variables (which means five coefficients plus an intercept, β_0). We might consider our regression formula to be something like this:

$$score = \beta_0 + (\beta_1 C_1) + (\beta_1 C_2) + (\beta_3 C_3) + (\beta_4 C_4) + (\beta_5 C_5)$$

In essence, we're saying that we predict the score on the placement exam —which will exist as a point on a regression line —to be the sum of each class's final grade (represented by C_1 through C_5) multiplied by their own individual coefficient (represented by β). It is through the process of multiple regression that we find just what those coefficients are. Are you ready for the fun part?

Since we're going to be using R for all of this, we will perform the multiple regression in one simple command. And in case you were wondering: yes, this chapter will be significantly shorter than the last one.

If you remember the practical application section in the chapter on simple linear regression (page 64), then you'll be familiar with how we developed a linear model with R's lm function. To use it, we simply specify what variable we want to predict (the dependent variable) and the variables that should predict it (the independent variables). The format looks like this (but don't type anything into the console yet):

```
reg <- lm( DV ~ IV1 + IV2 + IV3, data=ourDataframe)
```

For our purposes, the lm function takes a formula as the first value and the name of our dataframe as the second value. The regression variable can be anything; I named the regression variable *reg* so that it's easy to follow along. The formula for lm is constructed by indicating the dependent variable's name (which will be the name of the header row of the column we are trying to predict) followed by a tilde (∼), and then a list of independent variables that we wish to predict the dependent variable by.[39]

Since we're looking to explain the resultant placement test score by the grades in the pre-placement test classes, we will input the following code:

```
> reg <- lm(score ~ class_1 + class_2 + class_3 +

class_4 + class_5, data=withclasses)
```

It's fairly self-explanatory: we want to explain score as a function of (∼) each of the class grades using our withclasses dataframe.

When you enter the above code you'll have a new reg dataset. Now, remember all the math we did in the previous chapter on simple linear regression to produce our coefficients? If you type in the name of our regression variable in the R console, you'll have all of the coefficients provided for you.

```
> reg

Call:
lm(formula = score ~ class_1 + class_2 + class_3 +

class_4 + class_5, data = withclasses)
```

---

[39] Notice that we have added the variables "in the raw;" as we'll talk about at the end of this chapter, there may be cases when we want to square some of the independent variables or apply some other type of transformation.

```
Coefficients:
(Intercept)      class_1        class_2        class_3
 -4.653363      0.099925       0.202327       0.304415
     class_4        class_5
    0.007519       0.544334
```

There are two parts to this output:

The first section is located under Call and contains the function that created our reg variable. Below that, we see the magic section, Coefficients. Here we can see that all of the coefficients have been calculated for us, including the intercept coefficient. To create our regression line formula, we simply plug in the values of the coefficients. Our equation becomes:

$$\hat{y} = -4.65 + (.099 \cdot C_1) + (.20 \cdot C_2) + (.30 \cdot C_3) + (.00 \cdot C_4) + (.54 \cdot C_5)$$

Guess what? You just fit a model to your data. Congratulations! But you can't go home yet. Just because we fit a model doesn't mean our model is any good. The next step here is to validate our model by taking a closer look at it.

MULTIPLE REGRESSION DIAGNOSTICS

Just from looking at the equation alone, you should notice something very odd in one of the coefficients: class_4's coefficient is so small that when I rounded it to two decimal places, it disappeared into a zero. Recall from your first statistics class that as a regression coefficient approaches zero, it's effect on the dependent variable decreases. What we're looking at here is the very real possibility that class_4 has no linear relationship with the student's score.

We can learn more about our linear model by looking beyond just our coefficients and using R's summary function. You can access summary information on our regression model with the following:

```
> summary(reg)
```

The summary function will produce the following output:

```
> summary(reg)

Call:
lm(formula = score ~ class_1 + class_2 + class_3 + class_4 +

class_5, data = withclasses)

Residuals:
    Min     1Q  Median     3Q     Max
-0.6079 -0.1855 -0.0152  0.2298  0.5525

Coefficients:
              Estimate Std. Error t value Pr(>|t|)
(Intercept) -4.653363   1.834953  -2.536   0.0136 *
class_1      0.099925   0.004614  21.656   <2e-16 ***
class_2      0.202327   0.004259  47.510   <2e-16 ***
class_3      0.304415   0.004693  64.866   <2e-16 ***
class_4      0.007519   0.004383   1.715   0.0909 .
class_5      0.544334   0.021594  25.207   <2e-16 ***
---
```

```
Signif. codes:
0 '***' 0.001 '**' 0.01 '*' 0.05 '.' 0.1 ' ' 1

Residual standard error: 0.2837 on 66 degrees of freedom
Multiple R-squared:  0.9925,Adjusted R-squared:  0.9919
F-statistic:  1747 on 5 and 66 DF,  p-value: < 2.2e-16
```

There are a few things to consider in summary's output.

- The Call block that shows the linear model being summarized.

- Residuals shows us some information about our residuals. Recall from statistics class that residuals are the difference between the actual and predicted values of the dependent variable, or $y - \hat{y}$. Generally speaking, you want your regressions to be normally distributed, which would indicate to us that the mean of the difference between our predictions and the actual values is close to zero (and the closer to zero, the better).

- In Coefficients we have a bit more information than we did in our call to the variable by itself:

  - the Estimate column is the estimated coefficient, or, the value of the slope calculated by the regression;

  - the Std Error column represents the coefficient estimate's standard error,[40] which is the measure of the variability in the coefficient estimate;

---

[40]As a general rule, you will want the coefficient's standard error to be some order of magnitude less than the estimated coefficient.

- – t value measures the value to the model that the coefficient provides (hmm, class_4's t value seems awfully low...);

- – the probability that the predictor is not relevant (Pr(>|t|)) is in the final column.

- The Signif codes section is nothing more than a legend for the Coefficients section. You can see here that three asterisks (***) indicate a p-value significance of < 0.001.

- The final section summarizes some key test statistics, including our p-value and adjusted r-squared.

Take a look under the Coefficients section and try to determine which variable is not significant. It's probably obvious that class_4 is the odd one out. If you remember from earlier, we saw that its coefficient was rounded out to zero as well. What we're looking at here is a linear model that fits our data despite having a coefficient with a zero value. How weird is that?

THE *GVLMA* PACKAGE

The statistical part of your brain should be sounding the alarms. Is a linear model developed with a predictor that has a zeroed out coefficient a *good* linear model? Goodness of fit is certainly something we need to consider, which means we need to think about ways to diagnose our model. Thankfully, there's a great R package available to help us do that quickly and efficiently. It's called gvlma, short for *Global Validation of Linear Model Assumptions*, and it's going to make diagnosing our linear model very easy. Let's now go over some things we'll want to test and then how we'll test them with R.

There are four assumptions that a linear model must adhere to: *Linearity, Homoscedasticity, Uncorrelatedness,* and *Normality*. The gvlma package tests for all of these automagically. Additionally, there has been a lot of effort to compute a "global statistic" that can check for all of these assumptions at once. Pena & Slate (2006) created a sort of Neyman's smooth test[41] on steroids that accomplishes this, and exists inside the gvlma package as well. Thankfully, we can test for all four assumptions *and* this global statistic all at once with just a few lines of R code.

Inside your console, let's go ahead and install the gvlma package.

```
> install.packages("gvlma")
```

Your console will come alive with some indications that R is trying to install the package. Once it's completed, you'll see something like this:

```
package 'gvlma' successfully unpacked and MD5 sums checked
```

The next step is going to be to activate the library so we can use it. This couldn't be easier:

---

[41] Karl Pearson introduced the x^2 test in 1900, but it was generally considered inadequate for a specific cases. For example, when the deviations of the actual values from the predicted values are consecutively linear in either direction, x^2 takes into account the squared value of this difference, making the sign of the difference (positive or negative) impossible to account for. Because of this, Neyman (1937) introduced a a "smooth" test for goodness of fit, discussed exhaustively by E. Pearson (1938) in case you wanted to learn more about it. Alternatively, David (1939) provides a more gentle approach to the topic.

```
> library(gvlma)
```

Anytime you activate a package, you may get a warning that says something about what version of R the package was built under. You can generally ignore these warnings.

Now we have a new tool to use, so let's go ahead and use it. The gvlma package comes with a function of the same name that generates a really cool diagnostic summary of a linear regression. Since we have our linear regression stored in the variable reg, let's go ahead and create a new variable for our gvlma results given our regression results and see what our automagic test results look like.

```
> gvmodel <- gvlma(reg)
> summary(gvmodel)
```

Here is what the results look like:

```
> gvmodel <- gvlma(reg)
> summary(gvmodel)

Call:
lm(formula = score ~ class_1 + class_2 + class_3 + class_4 +
    class_5, data = withclasses)

Residuals:
    Min      1Q  Median      3Q     Max
-0.6079 -0.1855 -0.0152  0.2298  0.5525

Coefficients:
            Estimate Std. Error t value Pr(>|t|)
```

```
(Intercept) -4.653363   1.834953  -2.536   0.0136 *
class_1      0.099925   0.004614  21.656   <2e-16 ***
class_2      0.202327   0.004259  47.510   <2e-16 ***
class_3      0.304415   0.004693  64.866   <2e-16 ***
class_4      0.007519   0.004383   1.715   0.0909 .
class_5      0.544334   0.021594  25.207   <2e-16 ***
---
Signif. codes:  0 '***' 0.001 '**' 0.01 '*' 0.05 '.' 0.1 ' ' 1

Residual standard error: 0.2837 on 66 degrees of freedom
Multiple R-squared:  0.9925,Adjusted R-squared:  0.9919
F-statistic:  1747 on 5 and 66 DF,  p-value: < 2.2e-16

ASSESSMENT OF THE LINEAR MODEL ASSUMPTIONS
USING THE GLOBAL TEST ON 4 DEGREES-OF-FREEDOM:
Level of Significance =  0.05

Call:
 gvlma(x = reg)

                      Value p-value                   Decision
Global Stat          6.2729 0.17968    Assumptions acceptable.
Skewness             0.0199 0.88781    Assumptions acceptable.
Kurtosis             1.6123 0.20417    Assumptions acceptable.
Link Function        4.0654 0.04377 Assumptions NOT satisfied!
Heteroscedasticity   0.5752 0.44818    Assumptions acceptable.
```

A lot of that is exactly the same as our original call to summary(reg), which is R's internal model fitting summary function. However, starting about two-thirds the way down we see a new section: *Assessment of the Linear Model Assumptions.* The gvlma function automatically goes through and performs analyses on the four assumptions of linear regression and even the global statistic we talked about earlier. Let's talk about each of these normality assumption test elements individually, as multiple regression diagnostics is one of the most important things you will do as a social science researcher.

1. **Global Stat** As mentioned earlier, Pena and Slate (2006) proposed a global statistic that combined the statistical tests of Ancscombe and Tukey (1963), Cook and Weisberg (1983), Bickel (1978), and Anscombe (1961) in order to produce a singular method of globally testing all the assumptions of a linear model. You might think of this statistic as an averaged summary of each of the four linear regression assumptions.

2. **Skewness** is the measurement of the asymmetry of a random variable's probability distribution about it's mean.. This basically tells us the amount and direction (positive or negative) of skew. To be normally distributed, data should be as close to approximately symmetric as possible (i.e., it should have as close to no skewness as possible).

3. **Kurtosis** is a measurement of how "peaked" a distribution of a random variable is. Peakedness in a distribution is the height and sharpness of the central tendency relative to that of a standard normal distribution.

4. **Link Function** explains the linearity of the data. As Dobson and Barnett (2006) point out, the linearity assumption in linear regression means that we assume the response variable to be normally distributed; linear models can, however, have response

variables that are not normally distributed, which means that the relationship between the predicted value and the predictor values does not have to be of the simple linear form. For this reason, the link function is a necessary part in testing the linearity of a generalized linear model because it links the mean of the dependent variable to a linear term that can be used to form a linear equation to estimate the model parameters.[42]

From the output of the gvlma function we can see that the model violates the assumption of linearity (as evident by the Link Function not being satisfied). We already know that this is because, controlling for the other classes, class_4 does not have a linear relationship with withclasses. We can further investigate this by diagnosing our model's residuals.

RESIDUALS DIAGNOSTICS

The predicted[43] values in regression contain the portion of each observation that is explained by the model. We call the parts that are not explained by the model the **residuals**. Analyzing a model's residuals[44] helps us determine whether the model fits the data well, if we inadver-

---

[42]The link function links the mean of the dependent variable Y_i, which is $E(Y_i) = \mu_i$, to the linear term $x_i^T \beta$ in such a way that the range of the non-linearly transformed mean $g(\mu_i)$ ranges from $-\infty$ to $+\infty$. Thus you can actually form a linear equation $g(\mu_i) = x_i^T \beta$ and use an iteratively reweighted least squares method for maximum likelihood estimation of the model parameters.

[43]Remember that "predicted" here and throughout this book is usually synonymous with "fitted."

[44]Often called "residuals diagnosis" or "plotting the residuals."

tently left out any important predictors, and whether the linear model assumptions are satisfied.

Traditionally, a linear model's residuals can be diagnosed by simply plotting them. For example, if your residuals plot looks like a horseshoe, you can posit that you need to square the coefficient because the relationship between the coefficient and the predicted variable is quadratic and not linear. This method of residuals diagnostics works great when you have a single predictor but breaks down when you have multiple predictors.

Let's take a look at an example. Back on page 88 we created the reg variable like this:

```
> reg <- lm(score ~ class_1 + class_2 + class_3 +

class_4 + class_5, data=withclasses)
```

If we wanted to check the residuals of this model we could do so by using R's native resid function. By passing it a linear model, we will get all of the residuals for all of the fitted values. It's quite easy:

```
> resid(reg)
```

When you hit enter you'll get a screen full of data. We can visualize this residual data by passing the output of the resid function to the plot function:

```
> plot(resid(reg))
```

In your Plots window, you'll see the following:

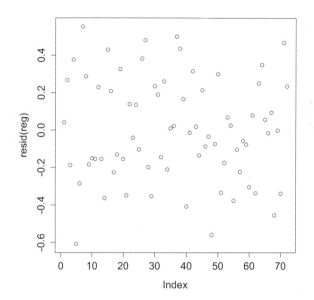

When diagnosing residuals, we are looking to ensure that there are no patterns in the plots. We want to see a plot that looks a lot like the above; the points should be evenly dispersed and not clustered around any single point, and there should not exist a noticeable trend in any linear or non-linear fashion. By the looks of this residuals plot, our model reg seems to perform well, right?

Not really. Unfortunately, by using the full residuals plot to diagnose our multiple regression model, we are not isolating any of the predictor variables at all. In this way, we would never know if one predictor variable is absolute garbage because it's just bundled up in there with all the other ones. So we're not really performing residuals diagnostics as much as we are verifying that, as a whole, the model seems to perform within expectations.

Instead of performing a big picture residuals analysis on our entire model, though, it's better to break down our residuals analyses into individualized plots that control for the other predictor variables. One plot per predictor, controlled for all other predictors. For this, we'll use the car package.

THE *CAR* PACKAGE

We can perform a more advanced method of residuals analysis by using partials residuals plots, or "Component + Residual Plots."[45]

To create Component + Residuals plots, we will use a second R package called car, which stands for *Companion to Applied Regression*. The car package will give us access to a function called crPlots(), which takes a linear model variable as an argument. We want to create component

---

[45] The linearity assumption can be checked by examining plots of E_j against each X_j variable, but these plots cannot distinguish between monotone and nonmonotone nonlinearity. To mitigate this, we use a Component + Residual Plot, which is a plot of partial residuals. The partial residual for observation i for the variable X_j is $E_i^{(j)} = E_i + B_j X_{ij}$, and we plot $E_i^{(j)}$ against X_{ij} to investigate nonlinearity. Additionally, we can plot the partial residuals against the partial fits, which are predicted values obtained from the part of the fitted model using only terms involving X_{ij}. These ideas can be generalized for models with interaction, for example, by creating separate plots for subgroups. Cook (1993) has shown that partial residual plots will correctly model the relationship between the partial residuals and X_j if either 1) X_j is linearly related to Y, or 2) the other covariates in the model are linearly related to X_j. The second condition suggests that by transforming covariates to linearize their interrelationships, we can improve the effectiveness of the partial residual plot. Generalizations of these plots have been suggested by Mallows (1986) and Cook (1993). For more, see Fox (2008) and Fox and Weisberg (2011).

+ residual plots for our regression in order to investigate its violation
of the linearity assumption by first installing the car package, loading
the package, and then finally calling the crPlots() function on our
regression variable.

```
> install.packages("car")
> library(car)
> crPlots(reg)
```

Once you hit enter on that last command, your Plots window in R
Studio will create the following image:

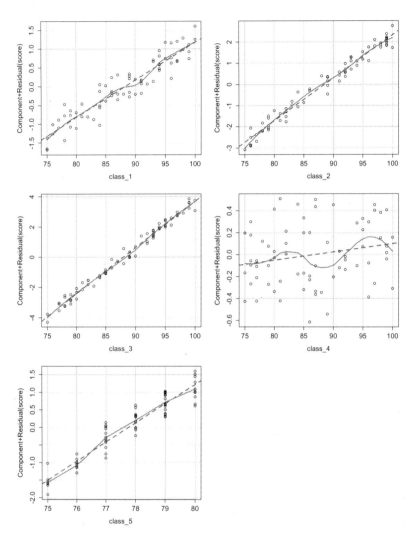

What you're looking at here are partial residuals plots for each of our model's predictors. Notice that each variable's residuals are normally distributed (significantly positively, if I may add) *except* for class_4's. If the plot showed something like a U-shape then maybe we could square the class_4 coefficient and make the function a quadratic, but alas, we have a big shotgun blast of data which tells me that we should remove class_4 from our model and recompute everything.[46]

So that's what we're going to do. Let's create a new regression with class_4 left out and see if our diagnostics confirm a goodness of fit. Our end-state here for a goodness of fit is two-fold: first, we want our gvlma() output to report that all linear model assumptions have been satisfied; second, we want our crPlots() output to show normal distributions (i.e., the lines should be close to each other and all the points should follow the line.

We'll create the new regression variable with class_4 omitted:

```
> reg2 <- lm(score ~ class_1 + class_2 + class_3 + class_5,
data=withclasses)
```

This will create a new variable reg2 with which we'll want to pass to both gvlma() and crPlots(). First, let's test the linear model assumptions:

```
> gvlma(reg2)

Call:
lm(formula = score ~ class_1 + class_2 + class_3 + class_5,
data = withclasses)
```

---

[46]When looking at a residuals plot, we normally want to see the "shotgun blast" of points because we don't want any relationship among our residual plots. However, with the component + residuals plots, we are incorporating a linear relationship test (remember when we talked about the Link Function on page 96?) so we *want* to see linearity.

```
Coefficients:
(Intercept)      class_1       class_2       class_3       class_5
  -4.27839       0.09889       0.20465       0.30527       0.54566


ASSESSMENT OF THE LINEAR MODEL ASSUMPTIONS
USING THE GLOBAL TEST ON 4 DEGREES-OF-FREEDOM:
Level of Significance =  0.05


Call:
 gvlma(x = reg2)


                      Value p-value              Decision
Global Stat          4.3677  0.3585 Assumptions acceptable.
Skewness             0.2871  0.5921 Assumptions acceptable.
Kurtosis             2.3350  0.1265 Assumptions acceptable.
Link Function        1.4728  0.2249 Assumptions acceptable.
Heteroscedasticity 0.2728  0.6014 Assumptions acceptable.
```

As you can see, by omitting class_4 we now have a model that satisfies all four linear model assumptions. You can see also that our intercept coefficient has changed a bit. Let's take a look at our partial residuals plots to double-check the normality as well:

```
> crPlots(reg2)
```

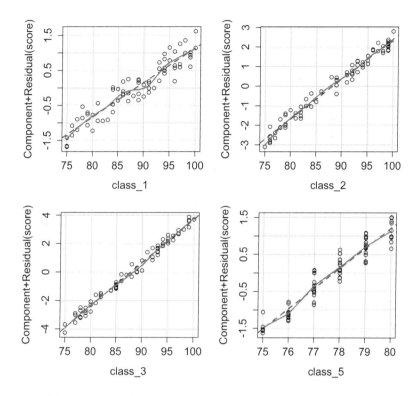

Would you look at that? We have a beautiful linear model that fits our data nicely, where $p < 0.05$, $R^2 = .99$, and our residual plots look great. Our final function to predict a student's English placement test score given grades from the four remaining pre-placement test writing classes is:

$$\hat{y} = -4.28 + (.099 \cdot C_1) + (.20 \cdot C_2) + (.30 \cdot C_3) + (.54 \cdot C_5)$$

We have now gone above and beyond answering the first part of the email from the student success center advisor back on page 82.

5.2.4   DEVELOPING KNOWLEDGE

We're almost done. Recall from page 79 that our hypothesis was that students who take the pre-placement writing classes have a significantly higher score on the English placement test than students who do not take the classes. To test this hypothesis, we'll perform a standard t-test on the means of each group.

To perform a t-test in R, let's first ensure that our groups are normally distributed since t-tests assume normal distribution. We can do this in many ways, but my favorite is with the boxplot() function. Since we'll want to compare the mean of the scores variables inside both the withclasses and withoutclasses[47] dataframes, what better way to do it than visually.

The boxplot() function simply takes in the sets of data whose means we want to compare, like this:

```
> boxplot(withclasses$score, withoutclasses$score)
```

When you hit enter, you'll see a pretty plain and boring box plot that shows the differences between the two groups. It's obvious here that there is a difference, and if we were to calculate the means of each group we could definitely determine a difference. However, box plots should not be used if the distributions between the two groups overlap too much because it would be difficult to immediately visualize a difference in means.

To clean up our box plot, we'll add some labeling to the output:

```
> boxplot(withclasses$score, withoutclasses$score,
ylab="Scores on English Placement Test",
```

---

[47]We generated this one back on page 84.

```
names=c("With Classes", "Without Classes"),
main="English Placement Test Scores")
```

Now our box plot looks like this:

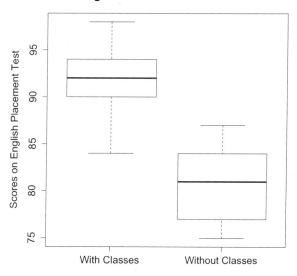

This visual comparison is nice for reporting differences between groups. As you can see, there's an obvious difference between the scores of those students who take the pre-placement test classes and those who do not. Of course, we can also compute the standard numerical summaries with R's built in functions.

You can compute the mean with the mean() function:

```
> mean(withclasses$score)
```

```
[1] 91.81944
> mean(withoutclasses$score)
[1] 80.73611
```

You can compute the standard deviation with the sd() function:

```
> sd(withclasses$score)
[1] 3.159276
> sd(withoutclasses$score)
[1] 3.928921
```

These are good to know but do not replace the t-test. Thankfully, R has also given us a the simple function t.test() for just this:

```
> t.test(withclasses$score, withoutclasses$score)
```

As you can see, the t.test() function simply takes the sets of data whose means we want to compare —just like the boxplot() function. When you hit enter, you should see the following:

```
Welch Two Sample t-test

data:  withclasses$score and withoutclasses$score
t = 18.6539, df = 135.747, p-value < 2.2e-16
alternative hypothesis: true difference in means is not equal to 0
95 percent confidence interval:
  9.908336 12.258331
sample estimates:
mean of x mean of y
 91.81944  80.73611
```

By default the two-tailed test is done and the Welch correction for nonhomogeneity of variance is applied. This isn't what we're looking for, though,[48] so we'll modify the function a bit to suit our needs:

```
> t.test(withclasses$score, withoutclasses$score,
alternative="greater", var.equal=TRUE)
```

We've added two parts. The first part, *alternative="greater"*, specifies that we're looking for the alternate hypothesis. Recall that our hypothesis was that students who take the pre-placement writing classes will have greater average scores than students who do not. The second part, *var.equal=TRUE*, tells the function to use the pooled variance[49] to estimate the variance.

When you hit enter, you'll see the following output:

```
Two Sample t-test

data:  withclasses$score and withoutclasses$score
t = 18.6539, df = 142, p-value < 2.2e-16
alternative hypothesis: true difference in means is greater than 0
95 percent confidence interval:
 10.09962      Inf
sample estimates:
mean of x mean of y
 91.81944   80.73611
```

---

[48] Welch's t-test is an adaptation of the Student's t-test, and primarily used to test the hypothesis that two populations have equal means when the two samples probably have unequal variances.

[49] Pooled variance is a technique to estimate the variance of several different populations when we suspect that the means of those populations are different *and* we believe that the variance of each population is equal.

The output is fairly straightforward: We have a p-value of $p =<$ 0.01 and a confidence interval of 95% supporting the alternative hypothesis that the "true difference in means is greater than 0." As it turns out, students who take the pre-placement writing classes are more likely[50] to perform better on the English placement test than those who do not.

With all of the complex analysis finished, you send all of this data over to Doug the Coordinator. Whenever someone sends me a list in an email, I always reply point-by-point, and that's exactly how you decide to do it too because you saw it that one time in that data science book you're holding:

> Doug,
>
> "1. I need to know which class has the least effect on the student's placement test score so that it can be dropped from the curriculum."
>
> *As it turns out,* class_4 *has the least effect. Go ahead and drop it.*
>
> "2. I would also like to be able to explain to the budget committee that participating in our pre-placement test classes will have a positive effect on English placement test scores."
>
> *The data you've given me indicates that pre-placement classes are strongly associated with higher English placement test scores* $(p < 0.01, CF = 95\%)$. *In addition, I can give you a pro-*

---

[50] Remember: Correlation does not imply causation. We can never be 100% certain about anything, but what we can do is reduce our uncertainty to an acceptable level.

jected English placement test score given the scores on each of the pre-placement writing classes.

It's that last part that's really going to hit home for Doug the Coordinator. Through the powers of multiple regression, we were able to develop a formula he could use to tell students what their English test score will probably be given their scores in the pre-placement classes. This right here is the heart of predictive analytics in data science; we are always seeking to find ways to describe our data in such a way that if we were given new information, we could predict the values of some other variable. Did Doug ask us to do this? No he didn't, but once we show him what's possible with a capable researcher like yourself armed with the tools learned in this book, he'll no doubt have more research requests very soon.

Multiple regression is, as we've seen so far, fairly straight-forward when juxtaposed with simple linear regression. The gist of their differences is in the number of predictor variables: simple regression has one predictor and multiple regression has two or more. Since it's still a type of regression problem, there are assumptions made when performing multiple regression.[51]

---

[51]This is especially true given that many multiple regression problems I've come across in higher education have exclusively used binary predictors. A lot of the research I do for community colleges involves student engagement. Generally, I'm testing whether a service used or a program executed toward a student population results in some desired effect. The independent variables in a lot of these types of studies are binary in that we record either that the student did or did not receive some services. I've chosen to use an exclusively binary dataset for this book's multiple regression example based on my experience in what people are researching. You can, of course, use continuous variables (or even a combination of continuous and categorical

For starters, multiple regression does not test the linearity of data; it assumes that the relationship between the target variable and each of the features is linear.[52] Another important assumption is that there is no multicollinearity.[53] Other assumptions include the *normality assumption* and the *homoscedasticity assumption*.[54]

In summary, multiple regression analysis is used when one is interested in predicting a continuous dependent variable from a number of independent variables.

---

variables) just like we did in the section on simple linear regression.

[52] For this reason it's extremely important to analyze the scatter plots of (Y, X_i) where $i = 1, 2, 3..., n$ and n is the total number of input elements. If any plot suggests non-linearity, you can apply a transformation (like squaring the coefficient in order to make the function a quadratic) in order to achieve linearity.

[53] Lack of multicollinearity means the independent variables are not related among themselves. This can be verified by calculating the correlation coefficient between each pair of predictors.

[54] According to Abdi (2007), the homoscedasticity assumption says that "the error is normally distributed and uncorrelated with the independent variables" (3). We talked about this a bit in simple linear regression on page 55.

Chapter 6

PREDICTING CLASS MEMBERSHIP WITH CLASSIFICATION

Earlier in this book we talked about the two types of problems that every problem can be reduced to: regression and classification. Recall that regression problems involve predicting numerical values, and that was the topic of the first part of this book. In this next part, we'll be focusing on predicting classification variables.

A classification variable is nothing more than a text label used to describe some data. Classifications can be ordinal, which means they have some sort order to them, or categorical, which means each label[1] has essentially the same weight. Data that can be classified easily is often said to have **linear separability**. Linear separability in data means that if you were to plot all of the labels of all of the data elements onto a graph, you would be able to draw a straight line through them.

---

[1] We sometimes refer to the class outcome variable as the "label" for which our "features" are used to make predictions.

Data that can be separated like this can be classified using a **linear classifier**.

There is another part to this chapter called **model selection** techniques. Starting with logistic regression and continuing through each of the classification problems, we're going to learn about different ways to select a model appropriate to what we're trying to do. Back on page 67 we were using things like R^2 to compare different models; this is fine for models with few and an equal number of predictors, but in data science sometimes we're looking to predict values using anywhere from one predictor to one hundred. As such, we need model selection tools that don't reward our models based on the number of predictors.

The first section in this chapter will involve the simplest kind of classification: logistic regression. It's the simplest because you just spent a good chunk of this book dealing with regression, and the outcome of a logistic regression problem can only be one of two possible value probabilities. It is in this chapter that we will also learn about two fast model selection tools: *Akaike's Information Criterion (AIC)* and *Cross Validation*.

In the second section of this chapter, we'll go over another popular classification method called a *Naive Bayes Classifier* (NBC), which will be our first (and only) foray into Bayesian statistics in this book. An NBC is basically a fancy way of predicting the value of something with respect to the likelihood of previous observations.

We'll wrap up this chapter with a section on *decision trees*, which are special botanical machines that you plant outside your office to gain extra special statistical powers. Just kidding; they're probably the more conversational prediction methods because of the way they create hierarchical rules with which to interpret your data and make predictions. When you inductively create a decision tree, you basically create a chart that someone can follow with their fingers in order to reach a (you guessed it) decision.

6.1   LOGISTIC REGRESSION

Hey, wait a minute! What is a regression topic doing here?

As it turns out, logistic regression is a type of classification problem. In simple and multiple regression, we sought to predict the value of some continuous variable given a set of predictors. With logistic regression, we seek to predict the output of a **binary** variable. Technically this is a classification problem because a binary variable can be either 0 or 1, true or false, up or down, etc.[2]

Feshoop! An email from the Dean of Counseling requesting a phone call. Suddenly, your phone rings. Honestly, I don't know why people bother to email if they're just going to call you anyway.

You pick up the phone and answer, and she's a bit nicer than she normally is.

"You know how we have program review coming up?" she asks, though the grammar fiend in you knows that she technically made a statement. "Well, we are looking to implement an intervention system to identify whether a student is at risk of dropping her or his current course. If we can come up with something, we can probably get funding for more part-time student service center assistants. Can you help us out?"

With your copy of Data Science in Higher Educationby your side, you confidently write back that you're up for the job.

---

[2] If you want to get super technical, binary refers to only [0,1], while any other type of two-value variables would technically be considered a dichotomous variable.

6.1.1 ASKING DATA-DRIVEN QUESTIONS

Here's some background on the Dean of Counseling's request:

Counselors speak to students on an appointment basis and, when they do, they collect specific information about that student to keep for their records. Student can be seen at any point during the school year, and data is collected uniformly regardless of who is seen or when they're given an appointment. The following table illustrates and explains each of the variables collected by the counselors when they see a student. Remember: the *feature variables* are those that we will use to predict the *target variable*.

Additionally, the counseling department has been putting together a theory about financial pressures and how they play into a student's likelihood of dropping. The following data is compiled after the counseling sessions are over and stored with the student data:

Taking a step back for a moment, you can see two sets of information here: the first set, which we might call the *customer's set* of data, is the data that the *customer of our services* (i.e., the Dean of Counseling in this scenario) has put together for our analysis; the second set, which we might call the *additional data to the customer's set*, includes additional information that either 1) we as analysts might find appropriate to include, 2) external stakeholders have requested to be included, or 3) a combination of the two. Theoretically you could collect an infinite number of data but it wont really be useful unless you're asking data-driven questions.

Additionally, you can see that this logistic regression problem has a few of our variables pre-selected for us. Namely, our target variable will be the binary dropped variable, which will indicate whether the student dropped all their courses for the given semester, because we

Feature Variables	Description
sampling_week	The sampling week (which is what week of class the student spoke to the counselor)
counseling_appts	The number of counseling appointments they've had this semester
classes_scheduled	The number of classes scheduled this semester
has_ed_plan	Does the student have an education plan?
is_online	Is the student an online student?
declared_major	Does the student have a declared major?
student_loans	What is the student's loan balance?
account_balance	What is the student's account balance with the college?
prior_drops	How many prior drops has the student effectuated?
credits_taken	How many total credits does the student have?
gpa	What is the student's GPA?
Target Variable	**Description**
dropped	Did the student drop?

Table 6.1: The feature variables we want to use to predict the target variable.

are concerned with determining what data can help predict whether a student drops. Additionally, our features have been provided for us.

Recall that the feature variables are those that we will use to predict the target variable.

To orient our efforts around a data-driven process, we must take into account that the counseling department has been theorizing about financial pressures and how they affect a student's likelihood of dropping. Given this, we might pose a research question like this:

How does a student's financial situation affect her or his likelihood of dropping all their classes in a given term?

Since we've added the additional data to the customer's set —which was, if you recall, elements that the counseling department was collecting as they theorized about financial stresses on student drop likelihood —our question should help guide our hypotheses going forward. This time, though, instead of proceeding with a set of hypotheses to test, we are going to be employing an inductive research technique known as *hypothesis discovery*.

HYPOTHESIS DISCOVERY

As you may recall from the introductory section on Data Science, *Asking-Data Driven Questions* requires us to formulate our research interests around the types of data that we seek to explore. A strong research question will imply certain types and sets of data for us to use, and by exploring research questions that are themselves data-driven, we can better inform decision-makers (and ourselves) with data-driven recommendations. Strong research questions, then, inform better hypotheses for us to test.

One of the things we may end up doing in institutional research is the opposite of that; we may be discovering hypotheses through the process of mining through data instead of finding or not finding support for existing ones. If you're familiar with qualitative research methods then you'll recognize this as a function of Grounded Theory, in which we use constant comparison and data analysis to formulate a theory that evolves as our understanding of data changes over time. Similarly, in discovering knowledge in databases we may only begin with a research question, only to discover a hypothesis through the very process of data mining. This methodology may be referred to as *Discovery science.*[3]

For many of my students and colleagues, this is the opposite of what has been taught. Traditional research would have us create a hypothesis and then seek to reject its null counterpart. In hypothesis discovery you still adhere to the principles of scientific research, but the process of reducing uncertainty shifts a little. Instead of performing deductive reasoning and arriving at a logical certainty, inductive reasoning is used to arrive at the most probable conclusion. This line of thinking is exactly the way we want to position ourselves because the very nature of making predictions is reliant on the probability of the model's results being accurate and not the logicality of the conclusion itself.

---

[3] Discovery Science may be defined as a scientific methodology which emphasizes analysis of large volumes of experimental data with the goal of finding new patterns or correlations, leading to hypothesis formation and other scientific methodologies. It is contrary to traditional scientific processes much in the same way Grounded Theory is in that we don't make any assumptions about the data before we actually work with the data. The fact that discovery science even exists imputes a new social phenomenological interpretation of data science and its effects on how we understand our world, but it doesn't present anything new. In fact, one could make the case that *any* methodology that would have you analyze data before hypothesizing and theorizing is just a modern twist on the Sherlock Holmes method of induction.

6.1.2   COLLECTING AND PREPARING DATA

We know the type of data we want to collect (from the table a few pages back), so now we just need to actually get it. As mentioned before, most of this data is collected by the counselors. Since we wanted to work with some financial data as well, we'll want to go to whatever management information system that our college employs and do a search by student ID. That should be fairly easy since it is expected that the counselors will verify who the student is (again, probably by student ID) before actually counseling them.

So we have data sheets that counselors fill out for each student in our data sample. Since they are collecting data already in their counseling and interventions process, we'll work with this information. That way, when we do give them a solution, they can apply that solution to the data they're already collecting and using. This is generally a good idea for higher education consumers because they tend to be more reactive than proactive when it comes to data management.[4]

Let's break the fourth wall now so you can download the CSV file that we're going to work with.[5]

Once you have it, go ahead and load it into RStudio:

```
preventiondata <- read.csv("prevention-program-data.csv")
```

---

[4] Please don't take offense to this (although if you're reading this book, I don't have to explain why I wrote what I wrote). It's generally not the job of non-researchers to worry about the nitty-gritty of institutional data, although something could be said about the shared responsibility we all have to collect, interpret, and share data about student achievement and institutional effectiveness.

[5] Go to lawsonry.com/datasciencebook, navigate to "Datasets," and find the link for "Prevention Program Data (CSV)."

Take a look at some of the variable types we'll be working with. Notice anything in particular?

```
> head(preventiondata)
  student student_loans sampling_week account_balance prior_drops
1          10071              5               0              4
2           1480              1               0              2
3           4701              4               0              0
4           2893             14               0              2
5           8785             13               0              2
6           2748              4               0              2
  counseling_appts classes_scheduled has_ed_plan is_online declared...
3                0                 0           0         0          0
1                4                 0           1         1          1
0                4                 0           1         0          0
2                1                 0           0         1          1
2                1                 0           1         0          0
0                3                 0           1         1          1
  credits_taken  gpa    dropped
24             1.26         1
 8             1.05         0
12             2.03         0
18             3.90         0
17             2.81         0
45             3.79         1
```

Right from the outset you should see that we are going to be working with several types of data. For example, *student_loans* is continuous, *is_online* and *declared_major* are binary variables, and some of the other ones are ordinal. How might we create a prediction algorithm that encompasses all these different data types?

One may wonder why we wouldn't just use discriminant analysis here since our outcome is either that the student did drop or they did not. As it turns out, discriminant analysis can only be used with continuous independent variables. In instances where the independent variables are a mixture of continuous and categorical, logistic regression is preferred. Logistic regression allows us to predict a discrete outcome (which, in our case, is whether the student dropped or not) from a set of variables that may contain any mixture of dichotomous, discrete, or continuous types.

Just like in our case here, the dependent variable is usually dichotomous. Another way to talk about what we're trying to predict is to say that the dependent variable will be true with a probability of success θ and probability of failure $1 - \theta$. In other words, θ = probability a student will drop, and $1 - \theta$ = probability a student will not drop.

An important aspect of logistic regression is that there are no assumptions about the distribution of the independent variables. Since they can be either continuous or categorical, they do not have to be normally distributed, linearly related, or of equal variance within each group.[6] Which leads us to the most important step in preparing our data for analysis: *categorizing our ordinal data*.

As you may have already noticed, the sample_week, prior_drops, counseling_appts, and classes_scheduled variables are ordinal, not categorical. This is an important distinction as there are few methods explicitly for ordinal independent variables in logistic regression. The

---

[6]Interestingly, the relationship between the predictor and response variables is not a linear function in logistic regression. Instead, the logistic regression function is used, which is the logic transformation of θ.

usual options are treating them as categorical or as continuous. Electing categorical will make them lose their order; what if one student had 4 counseling appointments and another student had 2? If, however, you elect for continuous then the program doing the analysis doesn't know that the variable is ordinal.

Let's think about this out of context for a moment. Suppose your dependent variable is "How much do you like the book *Data Science in Higher Education?*" and your answer choices are a Likert scale from 1 ("Very much") to 5 ("Not at all"). If you treat this as continuous then, from the program's point of view, a "5" answer is 5 times a "1" answer. Our whole analysis would be backwards!

To mitigate this, we must take a look at all of our ordinal data individually against our dependent variable to see if anything stands out. A popular (and easy) way to do this is to look at the frequency of distributions and eyeball areas where we can categorize the variable. Since we're all about simplicity, let's try to find ways to bifurcate our ordinal variable sets into two categories. This will turn all of our ordinal predictors into, essentially, binary predictors.

Frequency distributions can be analyzed using a histogram. Fortunately, R has some built-in functionality to display a histogram for us. Unfortunately, it's pretty worthless for our case and we'll use the ggplot package instead. Here's why we aren't using R's native function:

To create a histogram of, say, our counseling_appts predictor, we would do something like this:

```
> hist(preventiondata$counseling_appts, xlim=c(0,5))
```

The xlim=c(0,5) part basically says to limit our x-axis to 0,1,2,3,4, and 5, which will help our data appear a bit more organized. As you can see from your plot screen, the output looks like this:

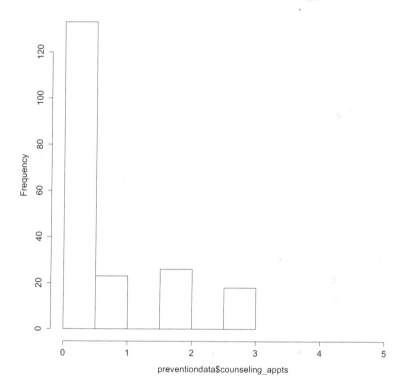

As you can probably already see, the output here is rather deceptive. It sure looks like there is something significant about students who do not have any counseling appointments, right? Could it be that students who do not see a counselor are more likely to drop?

Well no, but I'm sure some people are going to look at this like that. A frequency distribution like this basically shows the distribution of students who are part of whichever group. In this case, there just happens to be more students who did not see a counselor than students who did. What we need is this distribution broken out by whether the student dropped or not. Bonus points if we can do this all in one graph (hint: we can). ·

We can do this easily with the ggplot package. To display two histograms for the distribution of counseling_appts broken out by whether or not the student dropped, we can execute the following code:

```
> ggplot(preventiondata, aes(x=counseling_appts, fill=factor(dropped)))
+ geom_histogram(binwidth=.5, position = "identity")
```

Most of this is new, but that's okay. Learning by doing is the best approach to this. What we're looking at in a nutshell is a call to the ggplot function, which takes in the data frame that we want to use (preventiondata), then creates an *aesthetic mapping* (aes) which will describe how variables in the data are mapped to visual properties of geometric functions. In this case, we're creating an aesthetic mapping of two variables —x and fill —and then mapping those to a histogram object (geom_histogram). You can poke around with the data types to interchange them with some of the other variables, or even make changes to some of the formatting variables, like binwidth (which changes the width of the histogram lines).

Before you play around, go ahead and enter the code from above and see what happens. You'll get a histogram that looks like this:

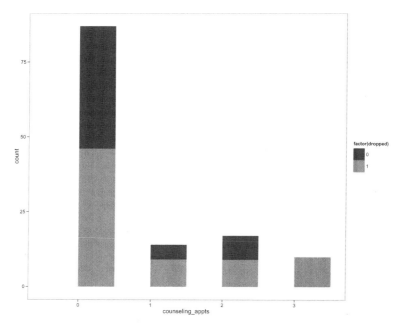

That's much better. Now we can clearly see the relationship between frequency distributions for students who dropped versus those
who did not drop —and it looks to me like there isn't really that big
of a difference. For the most part, it looks like a majority of students
did not drop and did not make a counseling appointment, but at the
same time we could say that the majority of students who did drop did
not have a counseling appointment. It's obvious from this comparison
of frequency distributions that counseling_appts is not a good ordinal
variable to split into two categories.

So let's look at another one. Maybe there's a relationship between
the week of class that a student is in and their likelihood for dropping.
We can compare distributions for the sampling_week by running the
following code:

```
> ggplot(preventiondata, aes(x=sampling_week, fill=factor(dropped)))
+ geom_histogram(binwidth=.5, position = "identity")
```

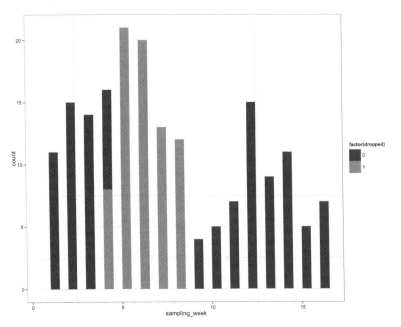

Well would you look at that? There is a noticeable clustering of the distributions for students who did drop during weeks four through eight. Could it be that students are more likely to drop during these weeks? That's exactly what this data says. Since the semesters are 16-weeks long, this graph indicates that students are dropping classes in the four weeks leading up to the middle of the semester. Hmm...

To help us test this newly discovered hypothesis, let's categorize this ordinal data into one of two groups. In the first group we'll put in all the students in a sampling week that is outside of this hot zone. In the second group, we'll put in all the students who did drop within this hot zone. To do this, we want to convert our ordinal predictor into a new categorical predictor. Let's call this new predictor in_hotzone, and we will assign a value of 1 if the student dropped within that week 4 through week 8 hot zone, and a 0 if that student dropped outside of the hot zone. You might recognize this as a form of *Dummy Coding*, and indeed that's exactly what we're doing here. One way to think about this dummy coded ordinal variable is that it simultaneously estimates a single "effect" of the ordinal variable together with a scaling of the categories that is optimal for this model. The resulting effect is sometimes called a "sheaf coefficient" (Heise, 1972).[7]

To create a new predictor in R, you simply declare the new column name and then assign a value. For example, we can create our new in_hotzone and automatically assign values of either 0 or 1 based on a condition we specify like this:

```
> preventiondata$in_hotzone <-
ifelse(preventiondata$sampling_week < 4 |
preventiondata$sampling_week > 8, 1,0)
```

Going through this part by part, we can see that we created a new variable in our preventiondata data frame called in_hotzone, and then assigned it (via <-) a *conditional value* using R's ifelse function. Additionally, our conditional clause included an *OR* operator(|). To better understand how it works, read the ifelse statement like this:

---

[7]The only real difference between traditional dummy coding and what we're doing is that I've decided to only create two categories; true dummy coding involves coding each ordinal component into a predictor, and in the case of 16-week semesters we would be looking at 16 new variables. To mitigate this, we're first testing our hypothesis about the 4 weeks leading up to mid-terms. If for some reason we discover that the outcome is not significant, then we can push forward and code each individual week. This would be highly unnecessary, though, as we can clearly see from the histograms.

if the sampling week is less than 4 *or* the sampling week is greater than 8, assign a value of 0; else, assign a value of 1.

The inverse of this is easy to extrapolate: *for any sampling week that is between 4 and 8, assign a value of 1.* After you run the code, reopen your preventiondata data frame and take a look at the last column. You will see our new in_hotzone variable with values for each row. Neat!

Now that we've cleaned up our data bit and even added an extra variable to play with, let's start mining this data for patterns.

6.1.3   MINING DATA FOR PATTERNS

Logistic regression is about determining how likely something is of being true. For example, with a binary target variable dropped, we want to be able to plug a set of predictors into an equation and then pop out a percent likelihood that a student will drop. To do that, we'll create a *generalized linear model* using R's glm function.

A generalized linear model differs from a typical linear model in that the latter assumes that the errors are normally distributed. As mentioned before, there are no assumptions about the linearity of correlative properties of your data with generalized linear models.[8]

Creating generalized linear models will look at lot like using the lm function for linear models that we used back in the section on simple

---

[8] If you look at textbooks or articles on the generalized linear model, the authors will almost certainly talk about the distinction in terms of the link function and error distribution. E.g., OLS linear regression is a generalized linear model with an identity link function and normally distributed errors. Binary logistic regression, on the other hand, is a generalized linear model with a logit link function and a binomial error distribution (because the outcome variable has only two possible values).

linear regression earlier in this book, with one addition: with GLMs, you include a `family` argument that is basically a description of the error distribution and link function to be used in the model.

To reiterate, the goal of logistic regression is to correctly predict the category of outcome for individual cases using the most parsimonious model. In our problem, we wish to predict whether a student will drop given the information that counselor's are already collecting. To accomplish this goal, a model is created that includes all predictor variables that are useful in predicting the response variable.

But which predictors are useful? We can get a quick idea of that by plugging them all into a generalized linear model function and seeing what we get. Let's go ahead and do that:

```
> fit <- glm(dropped ~ student_loans + sampling_week +
account_balance + prior_drops + counseling_appts +
classes_scheduled + has_ed_plan + is_online +
declared_major + credits_taken + gpa, data=preventiondata,
family="binomial")
```

Without going into too much detail, you can see here the fruits of our GLM usage discussion. The only thing that's different from the `lm` function that we used earlier in this book is the `family` argument, which we pass `binomial` to. We do this because when response data is binary, a Bernoulli distribution function is used —that is, the link function for our GLM is a logit link function, which is standard for logistic regression models.

Getting a summary of our data we can take a peek and the predictors we should concern ourselves with more:

```
> summary(fit)
```

```
Coefficients:
                    Estimate Std. Error z value Pr(>|z|)
(Intercept)        -1.183e+01  3.645e+00  -3.244 0.001177 **
student_loans       2.180e-06  1.742e-04   0.013 0.990018
sampling_week      -5.787e-01  1.688e-01  -3.429 0.000605 ***
account_balance     1.156e-02  8.167e-03   1.416 0.156776
prior_drops         4.524e+00  9.757e-01   4.637 3.54e-06 ***
counseling_appts    8.868e-02  3.501e-01   0.253 0.800027
classes_scheduled  -7.978e-02  2.801e-01  -0.285 0.775806
has_ed_plan        -1.581e+00  8.563e-01  -1.846 0.064846 .
is_online          -1.387e+00  8.816e-01  -1.573 0.115720
declared_major     -7.420e-01  7.976e-01  -0.930 0.352206
credits_taken       2.178e-01  5.241e-02   4.156 3.24e-05 ***
gpa                -4.539e-01  4.951e-01  -0.917 0.359233
---
Signif. codes:  0 '***' 0.001 '**' 0.01 '*' 0.05 '.' 0.1 ' ' 1


(Dispersion parameter for binomial family taken to be 1)


    Null deviance: 268.373  on 199   degrees of freedom
Residual deviance:  51.269  on 188   degrees of freedom
AIC: 75.269
```

The first thing you'll notice is that the footer block of the read-out says nothing about R-squared or p-value and instead has something called "AIC," which stands for **Akaike Information Criterion**. Pay attention to this because we're going to be touching on it later. Next, the coefficients section of the summary should look familiar. Looking it over, we can see that the sampling_week, prior_drops, and credits_taken predictors are significant to whether a student dropped or not. From the new predictor that we created earlier, in_hotzone, we already know that the week the student was sampled is significant. Is there a way to account for this?

Of course there is; we'll create a second model! Nothing says we can't create multiple models and then compare them to find the most appropriate one for our data. In fact, this is a very common methodology in data science; you always want to try out a few different ways to solve the problem before you fall in love with a single one. For our purposes here, let's take a look at the in_hotzone variable as a predictor in a new model called fit2.

```
> fit2 <- glm(dropped ~ in_hotzone + prior_drops + credits_taken,
data=preventiondata, family="binomial")
```

Let's take a look at how the predictors held up:

```
> summary(fit2)

Call:
glm(formula = dropped ~ in_hotzone + prior_drops + credits_taken,

family = "binomial", data = preventiondata)

Deviance Residuals:
    Min      1Q   Median      3Q      Max
-1.7914  -0.1869  -0.0395   0.1302   3.3876

Coefficients:
                Estimate Std. Error z value Pr(>|z|)
```

```
(Intercept)   -8.24288    2.08065  -3.962 7.44e-05 ***
in_hotzone    -3.11502    0.70504  -4.418 9.95e-06 ***
prior_drops    2.33614    0.47184   4.951 7.38e-07 ***
credits_taken  0.11885    0.03311   3.590 0.000331 ***
---
Signif. codes:  0 '***' 0.001 '**' 0.01 '*' 0.05 '.' 0.1 ' ' 1

(Dispersion parameter for binomial family taken to be 1)

    Null deviance: 268.373  on 199  degrees of freedom
Residual deviance:  61.559  on 196  degrees of freedom
AIC: 69.559
```

Two things should jump out at you: first, every single one of the predictors are very significant ($p < 0.001$); second, the AIC is number lower than the previous model. It would seem that by removing some of the under-performing predictors from the model we achieved a lower overall AIC. Without understanding AIC right now, we can probably assume that a lower AIC represents a model that is closer to the truth than a higher one. We can verify this by creating a third model using the original data that populated the *in_hotzone* variable. So instead of using our hypothesized (and subsequently supported) "hotzone" sampling week variable, let's use the raw sampling week and compare that model to our first two:

```
> fit3 <- glm(formula = dropped ~ sampling_week + prior_drops +
credits_taken, family = "binomial", data = preventiondata)
```

Notice here that our third model is the same as our second model, except we've replaced our *in_hotzone* variable with the original *sampling_week* variable. Let's take a look:

```
> summary(fit3)

Call:
glm(formula = dropped ~ sampling_week + prior_drops + credits_taken,

family = "binomial", data = preventiondata)

Deviance Residuals:
    Min          1Q     Median         3Q        Max
-1.63250   -0.09400   -0.00253    0.06830    2.97681

Coefficients:
               Estimate Std. Error z value Pr(>|z|)
(Intercept)    -13.72902    2.71500  -5.057 4.27e-07 ***
sampling_week   -0.45816    0.12817  -3.575 0.000351 ***
prior_drops      4.08407    0.80586   5.068 4.02e-07 ***
credits_taken    0.20004    0.04142   4.830 1.37e-06 ***
---
Signif. codes:  0 '***' 0.001 '**' 0.01 '*' 0.05 '.' 0.1 ' ' 1

(Dispersion parameter for binomial family taken to be 1)

Null deviance: 268.373  on 199  degrees of freedom
Residual deviance:  63.311  on 196  degrees of freedom
AIC: 71.311
```

Now we're at a point where we have three models on the table and a whole lot of summary data for each model. Our eyes are rightfully being drawn toward all those asterisks in the significance columns and we have noticed that the AIC is changing for each model. In the next section, we're going to take our analysis to the next step and start to perform model selection.

USING AIC FOR MODEL SELECTION

It would be difficult to determine, based on significance alone, whether a model is a better fit than some other model to the data because the idea of a better fitting model is entirely philosophical. As Burnam and Anderson (2004) point out, just having a criterion is not enough; "the first step [in model selection] is to *establish a philosophy about models and data analysis and then find a suitable model selection criterion*" (p. 262) (emphasis mine). We need to know what it is we are considering a "good fit" for a model before we can just go and use some criterion all willy-nilly.[9]

For our purposes, we're going to be using the **Akaike Information Criterion** (AIC) to help us gain some intuition about our models. In model selection, which is the process of comparing two or more models to determine which one outperforms the others according to some preset criteria, AIC is one of many different tools we can use to help us

---

[9]You see this a lot in higher education research, and when you do I would like you to point it out. Seriously. Ask the researcher, "why have you chosen that criterion to measure goodness-of-fit?" If they can't justify it then they should drop it. What I have noticed as "data science" has started to integrate itself as a staple buzzword among researchers is that we are still falling victim to the age old problem of understanding our data but not understanding the method with which we examine that data. For example, you'll often find studies reported with significance imputed by a high coefficient of determination (R^2), yet underneath this information is a model with dozens of parameters. (Just so we're on the same page, adding parameters to a model always increases R^2).

pick a model appropriate for both our data and our goals. As mentioned before, it's important to establish a philosophy about your models —e.g., the model that will be better fit will be the one that is most easily understood, or the one that produces the lowest of some criterion (in this case, AIC).

Coincidentally, that example is precisely what we're after here (hey, it's almost like I planned that!). Recall earlier our email from the Dean of Counseling on page 116. She wanted to know if there is any way to identify students who might be at-risk of dropping because she is looking to include in her program review a request for more part-time staff. Our job as analysts is two-fold: we must determine whether a model can be developed to help her in her duties, and we must also share that model in a form that is easily digestible. Which brings us to the rationale behind using AIC for model selection.

According to Burnham and Anderson's (2004) in-depth analysis, AIC is nothing more than "an asymptotically unbiased estimator of expected Kubric-Leibler (K-L) information" (p. 264). Put another way, AIC is a relative measurement of a model's performance against other models given the same inputs and the same target variable(s). Think about it as the amount of information lost when we use a specific model to approximate the real process of student persistence (in this case, whether a student drops). In framing AIC as a relative information criterion (hey, that's even it's name!) we can see that the model with the smallest AIC is preferred.

We can compute the AIC with the following formula:

$$AIC = -2l + 2k$$

Here, l is the maximum log-likelihood value of the data under this model and *k* is the number of free parameters in the model. If you're mathematically inclined (note: I am not), you'll notice that AIC penalizes a model based on how many predictors it employs. This makes AIC a good parameter for model selection when you are concerned with simplicity and coherence and want to avoid any resemblance of overfitting.

To get a quick summary of the AICs of each of our models, we can use R's built-in AIC() function:

```
> AIC(fit, fit2, fit3)
```

This will give us the AICs for each of the models in a nice little table:

```
> AIC(fit,fit2,fit3)
      df      AIC
fit   12 75.26945
fit2   4 69.55862
fit3   4 71.31119
```

Just so we're all on the same page here, *df* stands for *degrees of freedom*. Fewer degrees of freedom means the model has fewer inputs, but not necessarily that the model is a better fit. Taking a look at our output, we can see that the two models with the least AIC are fit2 and fit3. You'll notice that they both have the same number of degrees of freedom; they both have the same number of predictors. We can see here that two models with the same *complexity* have different AICs, which is a perfect illustration of when AIC comes into play when comparing models.

Something else we can see is that fit has 12 degrees of freedom. This is relevant for our model selection needs here because the other models have 4 degrees of freedom. If our goal in model selection is to produce a model that is both realistic and easy to use and deploy, then we would opt for the model with the lower DF. Lower DF means less independent variables means easier to explain (hopefully). In the AIC comparison table we made, we can see that more independent variables do not reduce the information criterion that we're using the select a model. In other words, *more variables attached to the model does not result in greater specificity.*[10]

So we can see that AIC is a *relative* metric to compare goodness-of-fit. Just like R^2 or any other goodness-of-fit criterion, AIC should never be used by itself to justify model selection. Instead, you develop multiple models (read: multiple competing hypotheses) and then compare their AICs to one another, making sure to consider the relativity of the degrees of freedom between models. For our example, it looks like we should be selecting fit2 because 1) it is in the group with the lowest degrees of freedom, and 2) of the models with similar degrees of freedom it has the lowest AIC.

---

[10] Oversaturation of independent variables also has problems in educational research when we see models reported purely with R^2 as the validation metric. Recall from earlier in this book that the coefficient of determination will always increase proportionally to the number of independent variables in the model. I can remember someone telling me once about this dropout and persistence model they made, and how excited they were because every time they would add a predictor to the mode the model would increase in "accuracy." Of course, this person was misusing the word "accuracy;" by adding more variables to a model, we don't increase a model's predictive power per se, but we can increase it's predictive specificity relative to other models with the same degrees of freedom. Remember: We're *selecting* models, not *measuring* them.

CROSS-VALIDATING OUR MODEL

Since we're performing predictive analytics, our goal is not to understand the phenomenon but to predict occurrences of the phenomenon.[11]

Now that we've selected an appropriate model based on the AIC, our next step should be to determine the predictive accuracy of the model. Careful, though: the idea of an absolute number that can describe how well a model performs against any amount of future unknown data is ridiculous. There is just no way for us to be certain that a model will perform a certain way given conditions outside of our control. While we can certainly plan for variations and changes in the data that we used to build the model, our best conservative estimate of a model's accuracy is not a number that we can say exists ad infinitum.

Instead, we can think of model accuracy as a snapshot of a model's predictive ability at a certain point in time. There are many ways to determine this predictive accuracy, but by far the most popular one you will encounter is cross validation (CV). Cross validation is a way of measuring the predictive ability of a statistical model. It's often used (and encouraged among statisticians) because traditional model diagnostic techniques (like R^2, described earlier in this book) are not necessarily the most accurate ways to measure the effectiveness of

---

[11]This doesn't relieve you of your responsibility as a social scientist to dive into the aspects of your study that you don't understand, but I do realize that not always do we have the time or wherewithal to turn every request for data into a full-fledged research study. That being said, we do have a responsibility as researchers to extrapolate and continuously add to our body of knowledge. Even if no one needs to know what we find out right then and there, at some point a future piece of data will be interpreted differently (and hopefully more truer sociologically) because of your commitment to seeking out understanding not only the *what* but also the *how* and *why*.

increasingly complex models. An example of this is the fact that I can add more higher-order terms to a polynomial regression model to increase the R^2, but in doing so I do nothing for the predictive abilities of the model —in fact, I probably made it worse!

In cross validation, we ascribe validity to our model based on its average predictive performance on multiple chunks of input data. Since it would be very time consuming to generate a model and then wait around for enough new input to validate the model,[12] we simply break up the existing data into sets of *training* data and then try to predict a target variable inside a set of *test* data. How many training sets we have are dependent on the flavor of CV that we use.

The simplest form of cross validation is called k-fold Cross Validation (k-CV). It's got that k there because we split up our data into k groups of training and testing data. Proper k-CV will ensure that the model that we developed stands up to different input elements that develop it, and is not biased toward a specific pattern or group of training inputs that may or may not accurately reflect the entirety of the dataset.[13]

---

[12] New data should still be used to sharpen the model as much as possible. Ideally, after deploying a model into use, new data should attempt to "break" the model —i.e., as the total amount of data that has been used to generate a model changes over time, so too should the model itself. In the example we're using in this chapter, what if some outside variables or aspect of higher education caused the sampling week to no longer be a factor in the prediction of dropout behavior? Unless you were routinely recalculating your models you would never be privy to these types of changes.

[13] Does this sound familiar? Cross-validation is a lot like experiment replication. The only difference is that with f-CV we are actually validating our models by attempting to duplicate predictive accuracy with different inputs; in traditional research, results are usually published without any attempt at

Let's take a step back for a moment. When we say "a model" we refer to a particular method for describing how some input data relates to what we are trying to predict. We don't generally refer to particular instances of that method as different models. For example, you might say, "I have a linear regression model" but you wouldn't call two different sets of the trained coefficients different models. When you perform k-fold Cross Validation, you are testing how well your model is able to get trained by some data and then predict data it hasn't seen. We use cross validation for this because if you train using all the data you have, you have none left for testing. You could do this once, say by using 80% of the data to train and 20% to test, but what if the 20% you happened to pick to test happens to contain a bunch of points that are particularly easy (or particularly hard) to predict?

How many groups we split our data into is dependent on what we're trying to accomplish and the overall sample size that we've compiled. The smallest amount of data you can use is one element, which is a basic version of cross validation called *Leave One Out Cross Validation* (LOOCV). Here, a single row of data is set aside as the test set and the rest of the model is used to train the model. Some people choose to use a set percentage of their sample size, like 90% for training and testing against chunks of 10%. As you can probably guess by now, determining the number of folds in cross validation is a subjective practice involving a lot of unwritten rules that need not be rigorously followed for the best result (Anguita et al., 2012).

For sampling sizes that are nice rounded numbers, I'll generally use 5 or 10-fold cross validation. I do this really out of convenience, as I saw that it generally produces a good average between LOOCV and

replication. See Ioannidis's (2005) *Why Most Published Research Findings Are False*.

more optimistic fold sizes. Feel free to experiment with the number of folds to see how different your results are.

After determining your folds, a prediction is made on the test set based on the model, and the the resultant *delta* is used to indicate the percent difference between the predicted value and the test value. The delta is what we're interested in, as this is how we will report on the model's accuracy. Think of a model's delta as a way of describing its calibration error.

Despite my long-winded introduction, cross-validation is very easy in R because of all the packages that have been created to employ it. My favorite one is the boot library, which is a very popular library containing tools for *bootstrapping*. In machine learning, a bootstrap is a calculation of some model's function repeated over a series of times. There are several variants, notably the *jack-knife* (also called LOOCV) and the *k-CV*, which we're doing in this section.

Back in RStudio, let's go ahead and install our new library:

```
> install.package("boot")
```

When you're done, load it into our current project:

```
> library("boot")
```

The next step is to compute the delta for the model that we selected, fit2. We do this using a function inside the boot library called cv.glm, which is short for *cross-validate a generalized linear model*. It's almost deceptively easy: you simply pass the dataset, the original model, and then the number of folds. For example, I could do something like this:

```
> cv.glm(data=preventiondata, glmfit=fit2, K=5)
```

When you type that in, you'll get a lot of console output that wont really make a whole lot of sense. We're not looking for the hard computed values of the cross-validations; we're looking for the resultant delta of our cross validation function. To get this, we simply access the delta method of the function like this:

```
> cv.glm(data=preventiondata, glmfit=fit2, K=5)$delta
```

```
[1] 0.04084616 0.04039090
```

I told you it was deceptively simple. The output of the delta object has two parts: the first part is the raw prediction error estimation, and the second part is the adjusted estimate which is calculated by accounting for biases in the cross validation process created by not using LOOCV. For our purposes, we can just compute the mean of these two values to get our total error. Feel free to call this any of the following: *calibration error, forecast error, prediction error,* or *negative accuracy value.*

```
> deltas <- cv.glm(data=preventiondata, glmfit=fit2, K=5)$delta
> totalError <- mean(deltas)
> totalAccuracy <- 1-totalError
```

Go ahead and take a look at your model's error and accuracy now:

```
> totalError
[1] 0.04102377
> totalAccuracy
[1] 0.9589762
```

Pat yourself on the back. You just did some serious data science.

6.1.4   DEVELOPING KNOWLEDGE

As will always be the case, our final goal in the analysis of data is the synthesis of intelligence. Looking back at our original research require-ments, we needed to come up with a way for counselors to use the data they already collected to put in place a type of early-warning system. We used logistic regression via a generalized linear model to whittle down the predictors to only a handful, and then cross-validated our resultant model to determine it's overall effectiveness. If we were doing a legitimate research study for publication we would've defined our hypothesis as having a measurable outcome —something like, "Sam-pling week and the number of credits a student has taken before can significantly predict whether a student will dropout (< 5% error)."

For our purposes, let's just assume that less than 5% error in a model makes that model pretty darn good. That means for every 100 students that the model predicts as possibly dropping out there will be 5 of those students that really aren't going to be dropping out —or at least aren't going to be dropping out for the reasons we have identified. Since edu-cation is a human enterprise, accidentally reaching out to students to make sure they're doing alright and not thinking about dropping isn't a bad thing. If anything, imagine the extra word-of-mouth advertising you'll gain when your institution reaches out personally to a student to make sure they're okay. (You can't get that kind of appreciation for the human factors in our work if you spend your whole career reducing students into descriptive statistics, but that's a topic for a whole other book.)

At this point we have a workable model that we can give to the Dean of Counseling. We can tell her that she should identify the students who are in "the hotzone," which we discovered early on was the four weeks leading up to midterms, and have previously dropped a course.[14] Are we done? We are with the Dean's request, yes, but there are a few more things we need to think about

Caveats:

Can you have a model that's more predictively accurate than another model with a lower AIC score? Of course you can. Just because a model is more accurate than another one doesn't it's less complicated, though. In fact, it's often the other way around. AIC is a good way for us to have something other than raw accuracy in selecting models so that we don't just jump right at the one that's the most accurate. Our goal in all data science is the synthesis of knowledge out of the collection and analysis of data; this is not possible if we make our models overly complex and sophisticated.

When dependent variables are categorical, simple linear regression and the ordinary least squares method cannot produce the best linear unbiased estimator. For this reason, logistic regression is preferred.

---

[14]You may notice that I have omitted the student's credits taken, which was identified in the model to be significant in predicting dropout behavior. This is one of those esoteric nuances that I have discovered over the years when working with dropout data. As it turns out, whether a student has or has not taken credits before is less about predicting behavior and more about tailoring intervention strategies. A student who has taken previous classes and is in the hotzone by receive retention intervention responses, and a student who has taken none or only a little may receive an intervention more closely related to a matriculation message rather than a persistence message —that is, a student who is having trouble persisteing would propbably get a call from a tutor and a student who is having trouble in their first course may get a call from a counselor. (Of course, this assumes that colleges really do care about student persistence and don't just sit back and say things like, "well, if they want help then they can schedule an appointment.")

Chapter 7

NAIVE BAYES CLASSIFICATION

How do we know that putting a cactus in our pocket would hurt? Most people haven't placed a cactus in their pockets, so we're not relying on actual experience. Instead, we infer the experience based on how we've classified observed (and hypothetically observed) actions. We know that a cactus has prickly needle-like spines; we know that our pockets are close to our skin; we know that sharp objects penetrating our clothes and puncturing our skin would hurt; we know putting a cactus in our pocket would be painful.

Interestingly, we might think of these sets of assumptions as naive because they can exist independent of each other. The sharpness of a cactus's needle has nothing to do with the proximity of our skin to the inside of our pockets. If we think about how our mind classifies things so that we would perceive of it as *painful* or *not painful*, then we're already thinking in terms of Naïve Bayes Classifiers (NBCs).

Our first peek at a more advanced form of classification will be with a widely-used linear classifier called the *Naïve Bayes Classifier (NBC)*. As a consultant over the years, I have found that NBCs perform very well and with a comparable accuracy to linear discriminant analysis and CART/CHAID[1] in many cases where we don't necessarily care about the interdependence of the predictors. NBCs work well for predictive analytics because:

- all of the variables in a system of data are used simultaneously

- you don't have to dichotomize variables or treat ordinal variables as cardinal ones

- they gracefully degrade when one or more predictor is missing or isn't observed[2]

Naive Bayes Classifiers really are cool; Zhang (2004), who wrote a paper fervently arguing for NBC's superiority among classifiers, calls them "one of the most efficient and effective inductive learning algorithms for machine learning and data mining." Hand and Yu (2001) reaffirmed the power of the "Idiot Bayes" classifier, owing much of its strengths to the way it treats predictors as wholly independent of each other. If you want an example of NBCs in real life, look no further than your email system's spam filter, which computes the probability that a new email is spam based off of previous observations of spam emails.

In higher education —and because machine learning is still so young in our field —NBCs are still being experimented with to help

---

[1]CART, or *Classification and Regression Tree*, and CHAID, or *Chi-squared Automatic Interaction Detector*, are types of decision tree induction methods.

[2]This is important when comparing NBC to decision tree induction methods, particularly because decision trees will fail if an input that the tree relied on for classification is not present in a future set of inputs.

create what I can only imagine are early-warning systems for institutional researchers. Some examples include:

- Abu-Oda and El-Halees (2015) NBC predicted dropout behavior among ALAQSA University computer science students with less than 5% error.

- Er (2012) found NBC to be 83% accurate in predicting dropout behavior of online students at the Middle east Technical University in Turkey.

- Pal (2012) was able to predict whether first-year engineering students at VBS Purvanchal University in Jaunpur would dropout with 60-90% accuracy.[3]

I have selected these articles in particular because of their application to higher education and to my point about the infancy of data science and machine learning in our field. Additionally, modern machine learning studies tend to yield preliminary results, relying on small sample sizes and limited analysis time to impute the need for greater attention to student data. That means foundational scientific work, like replication, valdiation, and rigorous criticism, are key to the success of data scientist types in institutional research.

When you find yourself with a limited amount of data and a limited amount of time, building an NBC is an efficient way to quickly

---

[3] I was particularly interested in this study because Pal operationalized Tinto's (1975) withdrawal variables, but what I started to realize as I got toward the end of the paper is that Pal was applying a system created with American students on students from an entirely different psychological and sociological background. Can we operationalize American-based research findings into studies on student behavior in other countries?

understand your problem. Its strength lie in it being a fairly basic probabilistic model (hence the "naive" part); it imputes a probability of some classification based on a series of perceivedly independent features. For example, a piece of clothing may be considered a jacket if it has long sleeves and a zipper. (Notice, though, that not all jackets have long sleeves and a zipper!)

Bayesian classifiers use **Bayes' theorem**, which tells us that the probability P of a given that we have already observed b is equal to the probability of b given that we have already observed a multiplied by the probability of a then divided by the probability of b. In equation form, it looks like this:

$$P(ab) = \frac{(P(ba)P(a))}{(P(b))}$$

This can also be written in a more explanatory way:

$$posterior = \frac{(prior likelihood)}{evidence}$$

If you have a calculator, you can construct an NBC with pencil and paper fairly easily. NBCs are great for exploratory data analysis because they can be trained faster and with less data, and as such are less computationally expensive than other methods. When you're looking to quickly find out if there is some greater problem to tackle, NBC just might be the way to go.

So how do they work? Let's think about how we might determine the probability that a new person we just met at a conference is in fact an institutional researcher based on what they are drinking at lunch. The following observations were made:

Given these previous observations, what is the likelihood that someone drinking soda at the conference is an institutional researcher?

Drink	Researcher?
Soda	Yes
Diet Soda	No
Soda	No
Soda	No
Scotch (ha!)	Yes
Water	No
Nothing	No
Lemonade	Yes

Table 7.1: Drink preferences for conference attendees.

We'll use Bayes' theorem to answer this. The formula:

$$P(a|b) = \frac{(P(b|a)P(a))}{(P(b))}$$

becomes:

$$P(Researcher? = Yes|Soda) = \frac{(P(Soda|Yes)P(Yes))}{(P(Soda))}$$

So the Probability(of a researcher | drinking soda) = the Probability(of soda | being drank by a researcher) times the Probability(of anyone being a researcher) divided by the Probability(of anyone drinking soda).

We can look at that table to get the values for each of these probabilities. Since there are eight total observations, all probabilities will be $x/8$, where x is the frequency of observations of that particular variable. So let's understand our data: three of the eight people were researchers; out of those three, one was drinking soda; out of all the people you observed, three were drinking soda.

Now let's put this in a more numeric way: the probability of a Soda being drank by an institutional researcher is 1/3 (1 soda observed for the 3 researchers we observed); the probability of someone being a researcher is 3/8 (3 researchers observed for the 8 people we observed); the probability of someone drinking soda is 3/8 (3 soda drinkers in total). Given all this information, we can now determine the probability of some new person being a researcher given that they're drinking soda by plugging in our data to Bayes' theorem:

$$P(Researcher? = Yes|Soda) = \frac{(1/3)(3/8)}{(3/8)} = \frac{0.125}{(3/8)}$$

$$P(Researcher? = No|Soda) = \frac{(2/5)(5/8)}{(3/8)} = \frac{0.250}{(3/8)}$$

By taking our observations and deducing a probability using Bayesian statistics, you can now determine the probability that someone at a conference is a researcher based on what they're drinking. According to our model, if you see someone drinking soda, there's a 12.5% chance they're a researcher and a 25% chance they're not a researcher. Probabilistically, someone drinking soda probably isn't a researcher. Wasn't that fun?

Of course, don't actually go and try to publish these findings —even if they were actual findings from a real conference (and yes, someone really was sneaking scotch in with a flask). Our Naive Bayesian classifier relies on previous observations that are construed as independent, and just like any other model you must always be updating your deployed models to account for evolving data. This also means you need to have a sufficient amount of data such that new data is not radically changing the model's predictions, otherwise the programs you create based on those findings will also have to radically change. A good example of this is spam email detection, which will almost always use a Naive Bayes Classifier to determine which of the emails you receive are garbage. Since the content and strategies of spam email senders has evolved over the years, so to have the algorithms that detect them. Every time you mark an email as spam, the probability of a new email that looks like that email being classified as spam just went up.

You can probably tell that this is both good and bad for student data. Bayesian classifiers will give us a quick and accurate probabilistic model, but unless we are constantly updating our model and ensuring that the data we use to train a classifier comes from within our institution,[4] we might as well just flip a coin to predict whether a student will

---

[4]There are two major problems with the present climate of machine learn-ing research in higher education. The first is that the sample sizes are limited to the individual institutions that are producing the research; the second is that algorithms are often taken at face value, and deployed in the field without consideration for the "learning" part of machine learning. When you see a study that correctly predicts, say, student dropout behav-ior, you shouldn't concern yourself with the resultant algorithm as much as you should the methodology of algorithm development; the underlying psychological and sociological elements that are allowing that data to emerge may exist only for that sample population, or only for that department, or that institution, or that region, or that country (do you see what I am getting at?) All research in machine learning must be rigorously replicated in order to validate it, and until you have replicated a predictive model using your own institution's data you should be very cautious about using it to infer generalizations about your institution's unique student body.

do x or not.[5]

At the Planning, Operation, Oversight, and Preparedness Committee, the Director of Marketing gets your attention.

"We sent out a bunch of postcards in the mail last semester and collected some data based on whether those recipients applied to our college or not. This year, we have a lot less money to spend on marketing and need a way of ensuring that we're getting the best bang for our buck."

You ponder a moment. "So you'd like me to give you a histogram, showing frequencies of demographic categorical data given students who applied?"

The director shakes her head. "Not quite. See, we have a list of potential students for the upcoming semester that we'd like to send fliers to, but we can't afford to send fliers to the entire list. I'd like to know who on this list is most likely to apply to the college if we send them a flier. Those are the people I want to spend money on."

Nodding, you pull out your copy of Data Science in Higher Education and thumb through the table of contents, remembering something you read on page 154...

"Ah, yes," you say, "you'd like a probabilistic model. I can do that."

The director of Marketing smiles and tells you that you can email her the list of candidates as soon as you're finished. She adds, "You'll have the data by the time you get back to your office."

---

[5]When you deploy a model into the wild, you must continuously reassess and rebuild the model while you collect data. A model developed to predict student behavior last year may not be the strongest model to predict student behavior this year.

7.1 ASKING DATA-DRIVEN QUESTIONS

What we're looking to do here is an important challenge that even non-educational institutions have to deal with. How do we ensure that the marketing material we are sending out is going to people who are most likely going to take action? Marketing research tells us that it's more expensive to acquire a new customer than it is to keep one. Since one of the effects of a good grasp on institutional research is a smarter budget, it makes sense that the research we do for marketing does have a positive impact on our college's fiscal position —and ensures that our institution is spending taxpayer dollars in the most effective way possible.

Since this chapter is about probabilistic models, our questions are going to be inherently data-driven. *Given past observations*, we might ask, *what is the probability that a person with a given set of demographic characteristics will apply to our college?* Something else to consider is that this is a binary classification problem.

7.2 COLLECTING AND PREPARING DATA

Back at your office, you see a new email from the Director of Marketing. Inside is a CSV file, one that you can download from this book's website.

Download the data file (CSV) for this chapter by going to this book's website:

lawsonry.com/datasciencebook

Once there, click on Datasets, then click on the Marketing Data (CSV) link under the Naive Bayes Classifier section.

Once you have it, let's load it up in RStudio to get an idea of what we're working with.

```
> data.marketing <- read.csv("nbc-marketing-data.csv")
```

```
> head(data.marketing)
    age commute_distance   education marital_status
1 18-24               15 High School        Married
2 Other               14 High School         Single
3 18-24                1 High School        Married
4 18-24                4 High School         Single
5 25-29               23 Associate's         Single
6 18-24               16 High School         Single
```

```
  cars_owned family_size         occupation applied
1          1           2           Medicine     Yes
2          1           1      Self-Employed     Yes
3          0           1      Entertainment     Yes
4          0           1        Hospitality     Yes
5          0           1      Skilled Labor     Yes
6          0           1 Money and Finance     Yes
```

Every variable is a factor or a category, which makes this very easy. The big difference between what we'll do here and our example earlier involves the additional predictors. In a nutshell, instead of just having one equation, we'll have an equation for each of the predictors.

The variables that have been collected are as follows:

- age is the person's age group, and can be one of the following: 18-24, 25-29, 30-34, 35-39, 40-44, Other.

- commute_distance is the person's commute distance from their home to the college, represented in miles.

- education is the person's education group, and can be one of the following: High School, Some College, Associate's.

- marital_status tells us whether the person is Married or Single.

- cars_owned tells us the number of cars the person owns.

- family_size tells us how many people, including them, are in their family. For example, two people with a child would have a value of 3.

- occupation is the person's occupational area. For this chapter, we're using the ones that are popular around a specific college.[6]

- applied is our target variable, and can be either Yes, indicating that they did apply, or No, indicating that they did not.

In Bayesian statistics, these pieces of data are known as the *priors*, or the *prior probabilities of occurrences*. When we use Bayes' theorem to compute a probability of, say, someone at a conference being a researcher based on what they're drinking, the resultant probability is called the *posterior probability*. Knowing these new terms, let's get right down to it and start mining this data.

---

[6] If you're replicating a demographic data collection strategy that includes occupational information, please be sure to check with your state and county employment workforce office to get an idea of the jobs that are worked in your community.

7.3   MINING DATA FOR PATTERNS

In machine learning, it's necessary for us to segregate our data into training and test sets so that we don't create an over-fitted model that's biased toward the data we're going to test it with. To do this, we create a *holdout set,* which is another fancy term for our training set, by segmenting a portion of our dataset from the beginning and not using it until we're ready to test. You'll remember that we did all this using the boot package back in the section where we were validating our classifier model starting on page 140. In this section, we'll be using a new package called caret to build four NBC models, each with their own validation method.[7]

The caret package, or "Classification and Regression Training," gives us tools to quickly and efficiently employ a variety of validation techniques to the process of classifier generation. By using it for our Naive Bayes Classifier problem, we'll be able to train, test, and report our results very easily. Additionally, we're able to quickly create a new model using different training criteria to produce smarter and more reliable models.

Each time we create a classifier, we need a way to estimate how

---

[7]Why are we using so many packages? One of the most frustrating parts of R for researchers who are new to it is the sheer amount of tools with which to tackle problems. Every possible method has a package, and each package has its own nuances and esoteric requirements that it's often difficult to keep up. I wanted to include more than one way to tackle problems like validation because it is my hope that exposure to more than one will guarantee that at least one will stick. So just use the method that is easiest for you to understand, and when you start feeling limited, return to this book to get a feel for new ways to mine your data.

well it might perform on new data. How is this possible if we're not able to know the new data we'll be testing it with?

To get started, let's include our new package:

```
> library("caret")
```

From here, we'll create our four different Naive Bayes Classifiers according to each of four common validation methods: LOOCV, Bootstrap, *k*-fold CV, and Repeated *k*-fold CV. You may recognize some of these from back on page 140 when we were talking about cross validation. We'll be creating these by taking advantage of caret's trainControl() function. A train control function produces a control object that tells our training function (called train()) which validation method we want to employ and how we want to employ it.

Once we've trained our models, we'll use R's predict() function to make predictions on each model's holdout sets. To report these predictions and give us an overall idea of the efficacy of each model, we'll use another new function called confusionMatrix(). A confusion matrix is a nothing more than a table that tells us how "confused" our model was when trying to predict known values.

So for each model, we'll:

1. use trainControl() to set the parameters for that model's validation method;

2. use train() to train the model according to our control

3. use predict() to make predictions

4. use confusionMatrix() to report the results and subsequent model accuracy

Let's get started!

7.3.1   LOOCV RESAMPLING

LOOCV, or "leave-one-out Cross Validation," is the laborous process of taking one observation from your data and making that the holdout set, then repeating that process for every observation in your data. Though this is often easier to implement, Shao (1993) discovered that LOOCV can yield inconsistent estimations even for true models. Thankfully, we don't have to worry about this too much since *all models are wrong*.[8]

To create our LOOCV model, we create a special control object by using caret's `trainControl()` function and massing its `method` argument "LOOCV:"

```
> loocv.control <- trainControl(method="LOOCV")
```

Notice that our control object—and all other objects in this chapter—have the model name as the first part of the variable, a period, and then the object name.

Our next step is to train the model. We'll do that by using R's `train()` function, and pass along the fact that we want a Naive Bayes classifier with our control object.

```
> loocv.model <- train(
applied ~ .,
data=data.marketing,
trControl=loocv.control,
method="nb")
```

There are quite a few new things here so let's look at them individually.

---

[8]This is a concept worth Googling!

The first argument for train() is the formula. Recall that formulas in R have a left and right side: the left side is the dependent variable; the right side is the independent variables. We have indicated here that our dependent variable (the one we're trying to predict) is whether the student applied or not, and we want to build a model off of that given the probabilities of all of our independent variables working together. We specify that we want to use all of the independent variables by using a period instead of typing out each and every one of our independent variables. In essense,

```
applied ~ .,
```

is exactly the same for this scenario as

```
applied ~ age + commute_distance + education + marital_status +
cars_owned + family_size + occupation,
```

The second argument, data=data.marketing, simply tells train() which dataset to use. You'll recognize the trainControl() object from earlier in the third argument, and the last argument tells the function to create a Naive Bayes (nb) classifier.

Let's continue with the rest of our models.

7.3.2   BOOTSTRAPPING RESAMPLING

Bootstrapping is type of resampling technique that involves taking random samples from our dataset and using them to test our model. This technique is good for discovering a model's performance variance, as some samples may test more accurately than others. Consequently, this technique has the effect of not containing some data points because of its propensity to overrepresent some of the elements from the training set.

To create our Bootstrap model, we'll use the "boot" method for trainControl():

```
> bootstrap.control <- trainControl(method="boot")
```

The default number of resampling iterations is 25.

Next, we'll train the model:

```
> bootstrap.model <- train(
applied ~ .,
data=data.marketing,
trControl=bootstrap.control,
method="nb")
```

Notice that the only thing we're changing for the train code is which model we are training and which train control we are using.

7.3.3 *K*-FOLD CROSS VALIDATION RESAMPLING

A popular go-to resampling technique, *k*-fold Cross Validation splits your data up into *k* groups, and then iterates through and builds models while letting each subset take a turn as the holdout set.

To create our *k*-fold Cross Validation model, we'll use the "cv" method for trainControl():

```
> kcv.control <- trainControl(method="cv")
```

The default for *k* is 10 when using the "cv" method.

Next, we'll train the model:

```
kcv.model <- train(
applied ~ .,
data=data.marketing,
trControl=kcv.control,
method="nb")
```

7.3.4 REPEATED K-FOLD CROSS VALIDATION RESAMPLING

You can repeat the process of k-fold Cross Validation and then get a mean accuracy based on the total performance of each repeated iteration. Kuhn and Johnson (2013) have discovered that, for some cases, repeated k-fold CV makes the most sense. However, Vanwinckelen and Blockeel (2011) argue that repeated cross validation is not useful "when the goal of the experiments is to see how well the model returned by a learner will perform in practice in a particular domain" since "the reporting of confidence intervals or significance is misleading" (n.p.). This is because there is a pessimistic bias from there being smaller datasets with which to learn from, and combined with the use of a single dataset, any attempts to reduce variance are perceived as a "waste of computational resources." It's up to you whether and how you use this in the future.[9]

---

[9] As you're researching machine learning methods, you'll not doubt come across a multitude of discursive scholarship. Some experts over here say that you should you *this*; other experts over there say you should use *that*. Academics say one thing, then professionals in the industry say another thing. One book recommends one way, and another book recommends another way. What do you choose and when? The more you tackle machine learning problems the better you'll become at recognizing how to tackle certain types of problems. In the end, practice creates a special type of intuition that no one can develop for you except you. So keep practicing!

To create our Repeated *k*-fold CV model, we'll use the "repeatedcv" method for `trainControl()`:

```
> rcv.control <- trainControl(method="repeatedcv",
number=10, repeats=3)
```

You'll notice that we've also specified to use ten folds (number=10) and repeat this three times (repeat=3). The other models have arguments we can use, too, but we've opted for the default values for them.

Now that our models have been created, our next step is to make predictions and actually use them.

7.3.5 MAKING PREDICTIONS

For each model, we'll use R's `predict()` function to get a set of predictions on a dataset based on a model. The function itself is quite easy: we simply pass it a model and a dataset to predict, minus the target variable. How do we do that?

First we'll find out which column number the target variable lives in. There's a function called `colnames()` that gives us the column names and their corresponding column numbers:

```
> colnames(data.marketing)
[1] "age"              "commute_distance"
[3] "education"        "marital_status"
[5] "cars_owned"       "family_size"
[7] "occupation"       "applied"
```

The output here shows a numerical label for every odd column, and you read the output from left to right. We can see that our target variable, applied, is column 8. Remember that!

To remove a column from a dataframe, we use the subsetting feature native to R's data elements. For example, if you were to pass the data.marketing dataframe to the head() function, you would get all of the column names and the first six rows of data:

```
> head(data.marketing)
     age commute_distance    education marital_status
1 18-24               15 High School        Married
2 Other               14 High School         Single
3 18-24                1 High School        Married
4 18-24                4 High School         Single
5 25-29               23 Associate's        Single
6 18-24               16 High School         Single
  cars_owned family_size          occupation applied
1          1           2            Medicine     Yes
2          1           1       Self-Employed     Yes
3          0           1       Entertainment     Yes
4          0           1         Hospitality     Yes
5          0           1       Skilled Labor     Yes
6          0           1  Money and Finance     Yes
```

By subsetting our data.marketing dataframe we can omit the 8th column by only grabbing columns 1 through 7. We do this by using brackets (just like an array, for you programmers out there). We'll specify that we want to account for all of the rows but only the first seven predictors. We do that like this:

```
> head(data.marketing[, 1:7])
```

That subset part, [,1:7], tells R to give us all the rows and only columns 1 through 7 (1:7). Manipulating our dataframe like this is very fast and easy, and we can even remove the head() function altogether and just specify that we only want the first six rows:

```
> data.marketing[1:6, 1:7]
```

The output should be exactly the same for both using head() and for omitting head and specifying [1:6,] instead.

We can now pass our dataframe sans target variable to the predict() function, which, again, takes our model for the first argument and a dataframe without a predictor. We'll be creating a new variable for each of our methods that will store the results of the predictions:

```
> loocv.pred <- predict(loocv.model, data.marketing[,1:7])
> bootstrap.pred <- predict(bootstrap.model, data.marketing[,1:7])
> kcv.pred <- predict(kcv.model, data.marketing[,1:7])
> rcv.pred <- predict(rcv.model, data.marketing[,1:7])
```

7.3.6 VALIDATING

When you report the results of a supervised classifier, you generally will use a *confusion matrix* to do so. A confusion matrix, also called a *contingency table* or *error matrix*, provides us a quick glimpse of how "confused" the classifier was in predicting the correct class membership. For each fo the models we created, we're now going to take a look at their confusion matrix.

The caret package comes with a function for confusion matrices called confusionMatrix(), which not only gives us an overall accuracy of the model, it also gives us a lot of useful information to assess model performance. The function takes in two mandatory arguments —the predictions made and the target variable —and then a few other optional arguments. One of those optional arguments allows us to specify a "positive" class, which helps us use binary classification terminology like "true positive" and "false positive." We'll pass along the value of a positive from our target (applied) for a positive case (which is "Yes", that the student applied) so that any references to a "positive" refer to a prediction of someone applying to our college.[10]

Let's build a confusion matrix for our LOOCV predictions. Building one is easy enough:

```
> loocv.result <- confusionMatrix(loocv.pred,
data.marketing$applied, positive="Yes")
```

As you can see, the syntax for confusionMatrix() is fairly straightforward: you pass along the prediction results and then the target variable.

Now, let's take a look at what a confusion matrix looks like:

```
> loocv.result
Confusion Matrix and Statistics

          Reference
Prediction  No Yes
       No  254  72
```

---

[10] Correctly assigning a positive class allows us to also correctly account for Type I and Type II errors. Recall that a Type I error is a false positive and a Type II error is a false negative; if our model predicted that a person would apply but in reality they did not, that would be a false positive. If we don't assign a positive class explicitly, sometimes R will choose the wrong class to associate positivity to.

```
Yes   13 678


            Accuracy : 0.9164
              95% CI : (0.8977, 0.9327)
 No Information Rate : 0.7375
 P-Value [Acc > NIR] : < 2.2e-16


               Kappa : 0.7985
 Mcnemar's Test P-Value : 3.155e-10


         Sensitivity : 0.9040
         Specificity : 0.9513
      Pos Pred Value : 0.9812
      Neg Pred Value : 0.7791
          Prevalence : 0.7375
      Detection Rate : 0.6667
Detection Prevalence : 0.6794
   Balanced Accuracy : 0.9277


    'Positive' Class : Yes
```

Yikes —that's a lot of stuff! Thankfully, it's broken out into relevant sections. The actual confusion matrix is the 2x2 table in the first section with the Yes/No counts (remember how confusion matrices are also called contingency tables?).

```
          Reference
Prediction  No Yes
       No  254  72
       Yes  13 678
```

In the 2x2 table, you can see that there were 252 true negatives (top-left) and 678 true positives bottom-right. We use these numbers in calculating two important metrics, *Precision* (which we see in the above output as `Pos Pred Value`, and *Recall* (which we see as `Sensitivity`).[11]

The next section of output gives us the meat and potatoes: the accuracy and descriptive features about our model. Let's look at each element individually.

```
Accuracy : 0.9164
```

This is what's called the "overall accuracy" of the model. We'll use this to quickly compare this model to the others. We see that our model has an overall accuracy of 91.64%, which is definitely better than a coin flip. Something that you wont see here is the `error rate`, which is $1 - accuracy$. When people call their predictive analytics "forecasting" or something traditionally statistical like that, you'll generally see them also report an error rate or forecast error. You can report it or not; you're save to assume the accuracy is enough to know how accurate the model probably is.

```
95% CI : (0.8977, 0.9327)
```

Here we have the range of values for a 95% Confidence Interval (CI). This tells us that there's a 95% chance that any accuracy from a

---

[11] Earlier I mentioned that there are multiple terms for the same thing, and this is a good example of that. In fact, I'm looking at three different books and a multitude of journal articles as I write this chapter and there must be at least five different sets of jargon here. This is why getting into and solidifying one's intuition with machine learning and data science is so difficult; half of the time is spent just figuring out all the different names for each calculation!

resampling iteration will fall between the lower (89.77%) and upper (93.27%) confidence interval limits. A wider range tells us that there might be huge anomalous elements of data, or it might reflect a gigantic sample size that contains too much variance for this specific model (requiring us to go back and rethink our data-driven questions and how we approach the problem). Contrarily, a very tight confidence interval is generally associated with —though it does not impute —a more accurate model.

```
No Information Rate : 0.7375
```

If you ever produce a model that performs worse than 50%, you basically have created something worse than a coin flip. The *No Information Rate* tells us how well our model would perform if we just consistently predicted our positive value. In other words, if we just assumed that every single person would apply to the college, we would be correct 73.75% of the time. This gives us a little bit of disposition information regarding our market, implying that, in general, more people tend to apply than not apply. In contrast, a very low number would indicate that our market is not very interested in applying to our college.

```
P-Value [Acc > NIR] : < 2.2e-16
```

Here's our old friend, the p-value. Since it's so low, there is substantial evidence that the Accuracy of our model is greater than the No Information Rate, indicating a working model. If our p-value was higher, then we would be less likely to reject the null hypothesis of Acc > NIR, which would be that the No Information Rate is greater than the Accuracy. So a higher p-value than what we're comfortable with would generally be coupled with a NIR that's greater than or equal to the model's accuracy, which gives us a basically worthless predictive model.

The rest of the elements are ways to finely tune our model analysis that, for our purposes, will generally not be necessary to worry about. Unless you're crunching some serious data with hundreds of features and multiple categories for the target variable, you can focus your attention on the overall accuracy of the model. I would, however, like to talk about one of those elements, and that is Precision.

If you have high accuracy and low precision, that probably means that your target variable is more evenly split between predictors (i.e., there is somewhat of an equal chance that a random guess would correctly predict the outcome). These types of situations call for a reapproach to the type of data you're collecting, or an understanding that what you're trying to predict may not be predictable very well. This is important to consider when we're trying to determine if a mostly accurate model is also not a worthless one.

Since we're only concerned with the comparing the overall accuracy of the models, we'll need to pull them out and look at them all next to each other. You can access the member functions of our `loocv.result` variable by typing in the following code and pressing the TAB key:

```
> loocv.result$
```

You'll see a list of all the attributes of our variable. Alternatively, you can also type in:

```
> attributes(loocv.result)$names
```

The above will use R's `attributes()` function, which will tell us the names of all `loocv.result`'s attributes.

The attribute we're concerned with is called overall, which itself has it's own set of attributes. How do you think we might get those attributes? Try running this, and take a look at the values you can get in return:

```
> attributes(loocv.result$overall)
$names
[1] "Accuracy"      "Kappa"         "AccuracyLower"
[4] "AccuracyUpper" "AccuracyNull"  "AccuracyPValue"
[7] "McnemarPValue"
```

So loocv.result$overall has an attribute called Accuracy, which, as I'm sure you've guessed by now, will give us just the overall accuracy of the model.

```
> loocv.result$overall["Accuracy"]
 Accuracy
0.9164208
```

We'll want to do this for each of our models to compare their accuracies.

Let's build the confusion matrices for the rest of the models:

```
> bootstrap.result <- confusionMatrix(bootstrap.pred,
data.marketing$applied)
> kcv.result <- confusionMatrix(kcv.pred, data.marketing$applied)
> rcv.result <- confusionMatrix(rcv.pred, data.marketing$applied)
```

With each of our models built, we can now go ahead and compare them. I like to use console output to quickly report information, and we can do that by creating a new data frame that only holds our model names and their accuracies:

```
> models <- c("LOOCV", "bootstrap", "kcv", "rcv")
> accuracy <- c(round(loocv.result$overall["Accuracy"], 3),
                round(bootstrap.result$overall["Accuracy"], 3),
                round(kcv.result$overall["Accuracy"], 3),
                round(rcv.result$overall["Accuracy"], 3))
```

You'll notice here that I've simply paired up a set of labels (the model names) with a set of model results, and for each model result I have used R's round() function to give me 3 decimal points of accuracy.

Finally, we'll stuff these into a new data frame:

```
> accy <- data.frame(models,accuracy)
```

And don't forget to call that data frame to get its values:

```
> accy
      models  accuracy
1      LOOCV 0.9164208
2  bootstrap 0.9164208
3        kcv 0.9164208
4        rcv 0.9164208
```

Well would you look at that. Each resampling method produced the same accuracy. Can you guess why? If you guessed that it's because the models are all binary classifiers then you guessed right. There's also another thing going on here, and that is that there's only so many ways to break up and test the limited amount of data we have. (Yes, a thousand or so rows of data is very, very tiny). So what do we walk away with?

To start, we should recognize that even with very advanced tools like the resampling methods we worked with in this chapter, datasets that aren't "big data" (i.e., millions of elements of information) probably aren't going to produce models that are extremely contestable. In my experience, you'll either get something that's usable or not. Only you can define what your acceptance threshold is, but I'm almost certain that if you generated a model with an accuracy like the one above you would be employing it tomorrow (assuming you can get it past committee, of course).

Machine learning is a vastly complex process, but the results for the types of datasets we're probably going to be working with in higher education will not require advanced methods of analysis to come up with good decision recommendations. If we had more data, and if we had a few more different types of outcomes, there is a good chance that we would come up with different accuracy outcomes for our resampling methods. In the end, though, most colleges would be comfortable with deploying a model in the 90% range just as much as they would be deploying a model in the 60% range.[12]

---

[12] This is purely from experience, and it's very possible that outside of California colleges are deploying predictive models that only meet a certain criteria. More often than not, though, the accuracy needed for a model to be considered deployable is rarely over 70%, which either speaks to the impulsive nature of higher education administrators when it comes to employing data-driven decision-making tools *or* it tells us that we can't really create hyper-accurate models when it comes to human behavior. Which do you think is the case, or do you have something else to offer? Send me an email and let's talk!)

7.4   DEVELOPING KNOWLEDGE

Our models wouldn't be very effective unless they're actually doing some predicting. With our new predictive model we can safely estimate whether someone contacted by marketing would enroll or not. We do this by taking new data outside our training and test sets and running it through our model.

We can ask our model the likelihood of someone contacted subsequently enrolling by building an array that contains the data describing the person whose behavior we want to predict. For example, let's say we have looked at a person on marketing's list of new prospective students (which means this list contains people that were not used to train/test the model) who has the following characteristics:

```
> prospect <- data.frame(age=c("18-24"), commute_distance=c(10),
education=c("High School"), marital_status=c("Single"),
cars_owned=c(1), family_size=c(1), occupation=c("Unemployed") )
```

We can use the predict() function to use a model and a new dataframe (which, in this case, only contains one person) to predict the likelihood of applying.

```
> predict(loocv.model, prospect)
```

The results of this will be a simple prediction:

```
[1] Yes
Levels: No Yes
```

This returns one row with the result, Yes. So an 18-24 year old unemployed and single person who owns a car and lives by themselves within a 10-mile commute of the college will probably apply to your college if you send out a marketing instrument. Neat! Go ahead and change some of the values for the prospect data frame and see how the prediction changes based on the inputs. It's really that simple!

Have we learned anything new about our data? With a predictive model as accurate as ours, we sure hope so! We can extract some information about our student populations by plugging in different types of data into our model and seeing the probability of that student applying. For example, you can create a new dataframe containing all the same demographic elements except for one (for example, age) and then run the model against each of the rows in the dataframe to come up with a probability for each age group to apply —all the while controlling for other demographic variables. This could help you answer questions like:

- Which occupations for younger members of the community are more likely to attract applicants?

- Which age groups in our community are most likely to enroll?

- Are people from larger families more or less likely to enroll at our college than people from smaller families?

Can you think of some other knowledge about your institution you could develop with a model like the one we built in this chapter?

7.4.1 CAVEATS & DISCUSSION

How do we know if we should use an NBC? Djulovic and Li (2013) found that an NBC classifier was technically weaker than the other methods they compared it to, but in terms of identifying the most students at risk of dropping out it performed the best. What does this mean? The application of a particular machine learning methodology to a problem requires us to think about what sort of answer we want. Are we concerned with a higher predictive accuracy? Or can we settle for "good enough" and assume that some students we identify may not actually be at risk?[13]

For an overview of many cross-validation procedures accompanied with pros, cons, caveats, and discussions, see Arlot and Celisse's (2010) article.

Here are some questions you can think about as you start applying the skills you've learned in this chapter to your own institution's datasets:

- How does the accuracy of the model change when you use a different split ratio?

- How does the accuracy of the model change when you use a different validation method?

- Could the data differ by semester? I.e., are some services more helpful at different times throughout the year?

---

[13]We could do worse than reaching out and contacting a student who is doing just fine but that a model has identified as being at-risk of dropping out. Can you imagine the type of word-of-mouth marketing you would get if instead of spending $25,000 per year on a super data visualizer you instead built some simple predictive models to identify at-risk students, then spent that $25,000 on part-time employees and student workers to reach out to students and see if they can help them with something?

Chapter 8

THE ROAD AHEAD (AND LOOKING BACK)

"What gets measured gets managed."

–Peter Drucker,

Armed with the knowledge you've gained and the intuition you've developed in this book, I now have an opportunity to begin the dialogue about important topics in higher education that are of great concern to institutional researchers. One of my favorite parts about reading academic texts (even though though I would hardly call this an academic text) is getting to the part where the author talks about implications for future research. Since this book is not about methodologies so much as it is about you developing and strengthening your own intuition as a scientist, this final part of the book offers some of my perspectives on several important areas of higher education.

It is my hope that the next pages will inspire you to start collecting and analyzing data at your own institution, and that you will reach out to me and share with me the things you have discovered, your "a-ha" moments, your successes, and most importantly, your failures.

8.1   A SHORT HISTORY OF SUCCESS AND RETENTION DATA

Since the 1970's, institutions of higher education have been aggregating student persistence and attrition data in electronic form. Researchers with backgrounds in social sciences and statistics —and more recently, computer science —have developed many tools over the years to drive institutional planning with respect to student success metrics (Kovacic, 2012). Since student success continues to be a relevant and important topic for colleges and universities (Golino, Gomez, & Andrade, 2014), a strong understanding of its two components —persistence and attrition (Davidson, Beck, & Milligan, 2009; Metz, 2005; Park et al., 2009) —is necessary for institutional researchers to be effective in informing and driving institutional planning.

The way we integrate student success into our operations and the way we research it is incredibly important for today's and future researchers because of the increasing pressures on colleges from accrediting bodies to produce reporting metrics and data that reflects satisfactory levels of persistence, retention, and student achievement. This chapter explains what student success is and how it came to be by walking through a brief history of how the idea of measuring and addressing student success has evolved over time.[1]

---

[1]Most of this is written with California's community colleges in mind, but all

Historical and philosophical influences of student success can be traced back to Emile Durkheim's (1951) work on the sociological aspects of suicide. Spady (1970) and Tinto (1975) both drew selectively from Durkheim's thesis, which classified suicide into two types: egoistic and altruistic. Egoistic suicide is described by a social phenomenon of felt integration; "suicide varies inversely with the degree of integration of the social groups which the individual forms a part" (p. 209). Altruistic suicide is the result of an excessive abundance or lack of social regulation such that moderately shared group values would inhibit suicidal tendencies.

The stark difference between suicide and dropping out of college might be summed up as a lack of perceived future opportunity. Spady (1970) and Tinto (1975) both operationalized Durkheim's group integration variables, the two most translatable to college dropout behavior being the presence of moderate social structure and the effects of said structure on feelings of connectedness and integration. An amalgamation of weak social ties to the institution and an omission of felt-integration is became the foundational component of future analyses based off of Durkheim's original study.

Durkheim was a French sociologist, but his contributions to sociological theory drove scholarship in higher education in America until cultural shifts that were created in the wake of newly formed accreditation rules and policies. Sociology is still very much closely tied to higher education research, but today more effort goes into reporting quantitative metrics and descriptive statistics than into traditional, qualitative sociological research to understand today's student.

In the 1970s, the view of retention shifted from being a solely in-

---

of it can be applied nationally.

trinsically dictated phenomenon to that of an extrinsically influenced one. Research started to look at how the institution —and not just socioeconomic status and individual psychosocial variables —influenced a student's persistence. Spady's (1970) sociological model was one of the first of its kind, proposing five distinct factors that comprised a student's level of social integration: academic potential, normative congruence, academic performance, intellectual development, and friendship support. Dropout behavior was linked indirectly to these variables through two additional, intervening variables: satisfaction and commitment. Spady followed this model with an empirical study to operationalize these variables, the result of which showed that academic performance was the predominant associative dropout characteristic (Spady, 1971).

With the passage of The Higher Education Act of 1965, the federal government established the first structure for continuous and sustained federal grant and loan programs for students across the country. Colleges jumped at the opportunity to qualify at a way to provide their students a way to finance their education, and newly empowered private accreditation bodies struggled to develop metrics for determining how an institution would be measured, to what standard(s) they would be held, and how standards and policies would be enforced.

Higher education research remained steadfast in its sociological roots, even somewhat cracking down on previous models that were not well regarded. Rootman (1972) sought to create a theoretical model to "explain findings" among a vast array of "atheoretical" studies that have been "narrowly empirical in design and execution" (p. 258). His intention was to create a predictive model for voluntary withdrawal, citing Hill (1966) and Knoell (1960) as the impetus behind stratifying dropout behaviors according to them having either voluntary or involuntary drives.

His model suggested that actual personal fit and person-role fit, both independent of each other, have a direct causal relationship with voluntary withdrawal. Each of these variables are components of social integration among peers and social integration with the goals and objectives of the institution, respectively. Rootman's model has strong sociological implications in the study of "total socializing organizations" (p. 268), imputing one's level of "Role-Fit" (p. 267) in an organization as the result of a complex catalytic relationship between stress, strain, and withdrawal as a coping behavior (ibid.).

Tinto (1975) provided one of the earliest and most widely cited bodies of knowledge on dropout and retention theories. He criticizes theories up to that point for trying to describe behavior instead of explain, citing Spady (1970) as one of the few exceptions. Much of the research on dropout behavior has focused on describing predictive capacities of different individual and institutional variables, but even he admits that simply reporting relationships is not enough; He provides the following example: "It is not uncommon to find, for instance, research on dropout that fails to distinguish dropout resulting from academic failure from that which is the outcome of voluntary withdrawal" (p. 89). Coupled with what is often derisory conceptualizations of the dropout process, the majority of studies are limited to descriptive statements instead of contextual analyses.

Dropout behavior is likened to Durkheim's (1961) suicidal behavior, in the same fashion that Spady (1970) used to describe dropout behavior, in that one's level of social integration can be a predictor of suicidal tendencies. Tinto describes an educational institution as being its own "social system" (p. 91) that has a similar set of sociological influences; "namely, insufficient interactions with others in the college and insufficient congruency with the prevailing value patterns of the college collectivity" and "lack of integration" would presumably lead to lower levels of academic commitment and a higher likelihood of dropping out (p. 92). To strengthen his argument, Tinto sought to create a predictive theory that addresses why students dropout —and not just what similarities exist among those who do —with special attention to the bifurcated nature of dropout behavior. Tinto proposed that there are two types of dropout behavior: academic dismissal, in which grade performance is the obvious predictor, and voluntary withdrawal, which stems from a "lack of congruency between the individual and both the intellectual climate of the institution and the social system composed" by the student's peers, faculty, and staff (p. 117). A student's propensity to withdrawal voluntarily is a byproduct of their goal commitment and institutional commitment, the former being a function of "insufficient rewards gained in the social system of the college" (p. 117) and the latter being a function of the student's connectedness to where they are pursuing their goals.

American cultural influences on student success can be summed up as shifting toward predictability and shifting toward accountability. There was a change in higher education scholarship from being focused on explanatory research to being focused on predictive research. This was probably due to the increased confluence of corporate business management practices and higher education administrative affairs. In fact, ascribing business management methodologies and frameworks to the act of administering institutions of higher education may be imputed in the evolution of the stronger and more stringent accountability metrics. The culture of accountability can be framed as a byproduct of increasing demands from accrediting bodies, themselves responding to the American peoples' desires to hold colleges and universities more accountable. The result of quantifying higher education like one would a business has been a state-wide, institutional, and programmatic obsession with descriptive statistical deduction.

The 1980's ushered in the "age of involvement" for higher education researchers, in which enrollment management emerged as a practice and field of study (Study Group on the Conditions of Excellence in Higher Education, 1984). Bean (1980) sought to synthesize existing research on retention and merge it with research on organizational turnover to develop a causal model for student attrition. He looked at previous student attrition models by Tinto (1975), Spady (1970), Rootman (1972), and others, and developed a model with 23 statistically significant predictors organized into five broad variable categories: background, environmental, organizational, outcome and attitudinal, and intentions.

Perhaps most notable in Bean's synthesis is the regard for background variables as significant predictors of dropout behavior in his literature review. He cites Sewell and Hauser (1972), whose eleven resultant variables from a study on educational attainment yielded a methodological preoccupation with pre-matriculation characteristics; he examines Boshier's (1973) theory about deficiency motivation, which is an incongruity between a student's concept of themselves as an individual and as a student-component of an institution, and growth motivation, which is the inverse of the previous variable, to the internal, external, and organizational variables that lead to dropout; he likens Tinto's (1975) model to Spady's (1970) and seems to emphasize that a student's self-conceptualization is a key driver in determining persistence; he analyzes non-instructional entities and opportunity outside an organization as a driver for withdrawal (Price, 1975) with Fishbein and Ajzen's (1975) model for intent, attitude, and subjective norms in behavioral formation to offer support for institutional commitment and intent to leave as significant predictors of attrition.

Bean's culminating predictors include: background variables (parent's education, high school grades, achievement test scores), environmental variables (transfer opportunity, job opportunity, family approval, marriage), outcome and attitudinal value (practical value, boredom, confidence, certainty of choice, institutional commitment, major certainty, educational goals, absenteeism), organizational variables (close friends, informal contact with faculty, grades, memberships in campus organizations, curriculum (availability of preferred courses, discussed leaving with outsiders, discussed leaving with insiders), and intent to leave.

This is but a small representative sample of the change agents in student success scholarship. As institutions began to think and act more like a business, institutional research began to shift from a sociological, highly qualitative practice to one focused mainly on quantitative, statistical metrics. The contemporary impact of such a shift has resulted in research personnel focusing more on reporting than on researching, on the assemblage of data rather than on analysis. Exacerbating this is the parallel rise in computing technology and higher education success metrics that give way for research studies focusing more on the appearance of statistical validity than on statistics' goodness-of-fit as the sole method for explaining student behavior.

Davidson, Beck, and Milligan (2009) acknowledge that colleges and universities are looking more and more toward literature in strategizing enrollment and retention plans, and that findings from studies are often difficult to generalize across student populations in different institutions, regions, and states; "programs that reduce attrition at one school may have little or no effect when introduced to other campuses" (p. 373). Tinto (2007) made a similar argument, concluding, "We have come to understand how the process of student retention differs in different institutional settings, residential and non-residential, two- and four-year" (p. 4). Similarly, Metz's (2005) review of 30 years of research on college student retention pressed administrators and institutional planners to develop an intuition about the data for their schools, to treat their school's predictors as wholly unique to their institution, and share Davidson, Beck, and Milligan's argument against a one size fits all approach; "Instead, we advocate for individualization, both at the level of the student and the institution" (p. 374).

The student questionnaire study developed and tested by Davison, Beck, and Milligan yielded three statistically significant predictors of student attrition after controlling for standardized test scores and high school class rank: "institutional commitment, academic integration, and academic conscientiousness" (p. 373) were positively associated with persistence at some institutions, and for others, "social integration, support services satisfaction, and degree commitment" (p. 384) were the predominant predictors. Overall, the general order of predictive validity across all institutions yielded institutional commitment as the best isolated performer, followed by the combination of high school rank, academic conscientiousness, and academic integration (ibid.).

As institutions look ahead for methods and instruments with which to combat retention issues, caution must be taken in making broad strokes and generalizations based on published literature. Additionally, retention rates rarely point to exactly why students are or are not persisting, giving institutional researchers nothing but the powers of educated speculation in trying to better understand retention rate variances. Perhaps the largest takeaway here is that institutions cannot rely on studies of other populations, and that each student population will yield its own unique set of institutional data with which a college can develop a wholesome picture that is the best fit for that institution's personality.

8.2   HOW DATA IS BEING USED TODAY

Early in 2015 there was a group of researchers at Dartmouth who created an app called *StudentLife*, which monitored mobile (smartphone) metrics and then predicted a student's GPA (see Wang et al., 2014). When this news was shared among higher education researchers there was a lot of hype about possibilities and excitement toward potentially employing something like this on local campuses. Why?

Much of what I'm discovering in a meta-analysis project of student success research since 1951 is yielding strong suggestions toward quantitative, statistical analysis and technology tools being contraindicated for appropriately predicting student behavior. What I'm thinking is that sometimes we focus more on an issue needing to be solved rather than developing stronger ways to perpetually address them.

Perhaps higher education's obsession with quantifying students is causing some to forget that students are people —not raw materials that we can magically shape into a finished product. One way of looking at the "overquantification" of students is as a byproduct of college education commoditization, but in "Why we are looking at the value of college all wrong," St. John's College President Christopher B. Nelson argues that "education and economics are essentially incompatible:"

The maturation of the student —not information transfer —is the real purpose of colleges and universities. Of course, information transfer occurs during this process. One cannot become a master of one's own learning without learning something. But information transfer is a corollary of the maturation process, not its primary purpose. This is why assessment procedures that depend too much on quantitative measures of information transfer miss the mark. It is entirely possible for an institution to focus successfully on scoring high in rankings for information transfer while simultaneously failing to promote the maturation process that leads to independent learning.

It is, after all, relatively easy to measure the means used in getting an education, to assess the learning of intermediate skills that prepare one for a higher purpose —things like mastering vocabulary and spelling, for instance, which help one to communicate. It is also easy to measure the handy, quantifiable by-products of a college education, like post-graduate earning, either in the short term or long term. But both of these kinds of measures fail to speak to education's proper end —the maturation of the student.

Tools like a GPA Predictamicator perpetuate a Culture of Quantification Hype that encourage people to regard metrics and numbers as equipollent to the sociological roots of education research and the human part of a human enterprise like college. Think back to W. E. B. Du Bois' (1903) The Souls of Black Folk: "The function of the university is not simply to teach bread-winning, or to furnish teachers for the public schools or to be a centre of polite society; it is, above all, to be the organ of that fine adjustment between real life and the growing knowledge of life, an adjustment which forms the secret of civilization."

Looking at what the researchers are studying in the referenced material is actually pretty disheartening to me —not because of the tools and technology they're using, but because they're trying to come up with new answers to questions that have been answered for over a half of a century.

From a more positivistic perspective, can cell phones help us understand a student's lifestyle? Sure! But what actionable intelligence is this information contributing to? I mean, which should we be focusing on: What a student is doing in the next two weeks or why they're waiting two weeks for a counseling appointment?

Sampling isn't the larger issue with this study, though. When I see things like this come out I feel like they receive a whole lot of attention because we are always looking for the next big tool or piece of software to provide us with answers, when in reality we should be focusing on whether we are asking the right questions.

We don't need more tools; we need more relationships. Relationships between the administrators and the faculty, between the students and the institution. Tools don't teach. Software doesn't make a student successful. To quote the last sentence from the previously linked article, "Unless we stop taking the easy way, unless we get past our habit of interpreting everything in economic terms, we will never grasp the true value of a college education."

8.3   HOW ACCREDITATION COULD BE RE- ENGI- NEERED WITH DATA SCIENCE

When it's time to start preparing for accreditation, California community college administrators may be on edge because they are at a higher risk for sanction than any other community college in the nation (California State Auditor, 2014, p. 3). For institutions both large and small, getting ready for an accreditation review has become an exponentially burdening process of collecting data, analyzing trends, and reporting climates and outcomes inside self-study measurements designed to somewhat market the institution as worthy of reaffirmation (Shibley & Volkwein, 2002). State regulations stipulate that the Accrediting Commission for Community and Junior Colleges, Western Association of Schools and Colleges (ACCJC-WASC), a non-profit organization comprised of representatives from accredited community colleges, is the single accreditor of community colleges in California. This puts enormous pressure on a single entity to ensure to the public that each of the State's 112 community colleges are qualified to receive Federal financial aid, award degrees and certificates, and participate in transfer articulation agreements.

In addition to this, one of the results of ACCJC's monopoly on accreditation is that community colleges in California are guided by a single set of criteria when planning their college's processes. The ACCJC publishes a list of Accreditation Standards that are intended to serve as a springboard for institutional dialogue effectuated through a college's self-evaluation report. Ironically, there are no characteristically objective (i.e., quantitative) metrics with which to measure one's institution that directly pertain to accreditation preparedness, despite the overwhelming necessity for institutions to maintain their accreditation. Though the ACCJC enumerates guidelines for everything from financial planning integration to elements of a college's mission statement, the reliance on "qualitative opinions derived from quantitative data" (Roose & Anderson, 1972, p. 115) may render the process of self-evaluation —and indeed the accreditation process as a whole —as ultimately subjective.

Therefore, an opportunity to develop a metric that quantifies a college's accreditation preparedness presents itself. This metric would essentially be a *pre-accreditation strength score* that offers a quantitative component to the self-evaluation process, providing institutions with a critical, data-driven framework with which to address how well the institution 1) meets certain guidelines as set forth by a governing body, 2) compares to other institutions in the region, and 3) compares to other institutions in the country. With this opportunity comes the bifurcation of the accreditation process into two components: *assessment of the process*, which occurs in the traditional, self-evaluative sense of accreditation, and *assessment of the product*, which is the evaluation of how well a college performs the functions of a college.

The following questions are presented for further research:

What is a college's product and what is the best way to measure it?

The current process of accreditation serves not to measure but rather to explain, and without measurement there is no objective quantification of an institution's ability to meet its mission. How can we 1) define what an institution *ought* to do (i.e., what is their product), and 2) determine the best way to measure this product? In contrast, is this an appropriate way to measure an institute of higher education?

My assumption here is that there is a desire to have a metric or even set of descriptive statistics with which a college can base their self-evaluation. This is somewhat eluded to in my field notes generated through discussions with institutional leaders. These grounded theory approaches to collecting data on accreditation preparedness has yielded three overarching themes: frustration with the inability of academic leaders to accurately *predict accreditation strength*; the recognition of accreditation in its current form as *subjective* and thus favoring those institutions that have the capacity and wherewithal to perform rigorous qualitative assessments; the desire for *a wholly objective, peer-*

reviewed accreditation process that is separate from any one governing commission.

What quantitative metrics are used to evaluate institutions of higher education?

There are many different management information systems and data repositories used by higher education institutions, including, but not limited to: statewide repositories used by the offices of chancellors or other education leaders; district information systems hosted on site or through a third party; systems at the National Center for Education Statistics (NCES); the Integrated Postsecondary Education Data System (IPEDS); accreditation commission reporting data and data aggregation systems. Identifying these databases and determining what their efficacy is in the accreditation process may produce insight into whether current data collection and reporting processes are sufficient enough to build an objective picture of institutional strength.

As someone who works in research and technology in higher education, it is my assumption that all leaders are at least somewhat familiar with the data repositories that are provided to colleges and universities. It is also my assumption, however, that these repositories largely go under-utilized, as both experience and interview data has shown a disparity among the data collected and reported by institutions and the nature of college planning and program review. This alludes to an aspect of this topic that could have multiple interpretations, as what datasets should be used for what is highly debatable in many regards.

What quantitative element(s) could provide an objective link between federal funding and accreditation?

Accreditation is how the federal government green lights federal funding for colleges and universities. When the Higher Education Act of 1965 passed, requiring institutions seeking federal student aid for their students to have and maintain accreditation, the federal government implicitly endorsed self-regulatory accreditation bodies as being capable and trustworthy gatekeepers to federal funding (Areen, 2011). By working together, institutions and accreditors would assure the public and the government of academic quality accountability, and under these auspices, colleges and universities would be extended the opportunity to receive federal student aid.

Since a qualitative methodology puts more emphasis in persuasive rhetoric than it does in objective data (Smaling, 2002), the current accreditation process may rely too heavily on subjective analysis than on objective outcomes. At present, there is no metric available to give education administrators a clear picture of their institution's preparedness for an upcoming accreditation process. This results in a one to one and a half year focus on preparing for an upcoming accreditation visit; many leaders interviewed have expressed the desire to have accreditation preparedness to be an ongoing process, but have indicated that there are fundamental, institutional issues with doing this. Future research in the form of additional interviews or a survey could lead to insight about whether or not education leaders had anticipated negative accreditation outcomes and what an ongoing accreditation process may have done to address them. Additionally, data mining and knowledge discovery processes could help address the research challenges presented herein.

A central concern is whether there exists a set of aggregate quantitative data that could potentially facilitate a new accreditation preparedness metric. There is of course a personal interest here for all those involved in institutional effectiveness because identifying a new metric for measuring an institution's ability to meet the needs of its community as an institution of higher education would greatly enhance the accreditation planning process. In my own personal job, I end up having to rely on professional judgment in accreditation planning rather than objective measures, turning the accreditation planning process into an exercise in forensics rather than a reporting process. This is a problem in colleges across the country, with leaders from different schools often times at odds when it comes to interpreting accreditation standards. It is in this research challenge that the connection between how to plan for accreditation, what data we currently use for accreditation, and what data we should use for accreditation is imputed.

What is an objective picture of an institution is fuzzily defined at best. While field notes have yielded conflicted opinions on what constitutes success in a higher education environment, most academic leaders have agreed that *student outcomes*, defined here as the relative grades and performance of college students, and *student success*, defined here as the attainment of institutional student goals (e.g., the conferral of a degree or certificate or the successful transfer to a 4-year university), are paramount to judging whether a college should be accredited or not. I share this opinion and I think this perspective will aid in the discovery of how a leader's perspectives on the accreditation process shape her or his college's strategic planning efforts and operations.

My own assumptions on this topic reflect those of other institutional leaders: *there is an alarming lack of research on accreditation in the United States, necessitating greater attention to how colleges are preparing for accreditation and how accreditation planning drives college strategic planning as a whole.*

Additionally, since the ACCJC's high sanction rate may be due in part to its short accreditation cycle —six years versus anywhere between seven and 10 years for other accreditors —college strategic planning may require greater emphasis on accreditation preparation. The ACCJC does not provide feedback on a pre-accreditation institutional self-study, so institutions do not have an opportunity to address commission concerns before an external evaluation team comes in and performs a comprehensive accreditation review. A system that enabled colleges to assess their pre-accreditation strength would aid the strategic planning process and may even provide guidance for macroscopic planning effort.

8.3.1 INSTITUTIONAL SANCTION

In a report to the governor of California and state legislative leaders, California State Auditor Elaine Howle (2014) expressed several concerns about these harsh policies and practices. Four in particular stand out: First, it was discovered that, while the ACCJC describes its obligation to facilitating a transparent accreditation process, much of the commissions deliberations occur behind closed doors; Second, the process of appealing an ACCJC decision does not afford an institution to introduce new evidence âĂŞ that is, if the commission decided to terminate accreditation for an institution due to not having met a set of recommendations, the institution has no recourse to show that processes were in place and movement has been made toward the meeting of said recommendations; Third, a longitudinal study of all accrediting bodies across the nation revealed that the ACCJC sanctions colleges at a "significantly higher rate" than any other regional accreditor in America; Fourth, it was discovered that there is much room for improvement at the California Community Colleges Chancellor's Office (CCCCO) in terms of monitoring colleges across the state and identifying those institutions that may be at risk of sanction or even revocation of accreditation from the commission.

For many involved in the accreditation process, these implications may be alarming. For example, while over 80% of the institutions accredited by the ACCJC are public California community colleges subject to strict standards of process and information transparency than private educational institutions, the ACCJC does not post the process of deliberation with regard to possible sanctions on a college to the public. Additionally, only 62% of respondents to a statewide survey believed that the commission's decision-making processes were suitably transparent, which implies a shockingly high minority of respondents who feel that the ACCJC is not as transparent in their decision-making as they should me (California State Auditor, 2014, p. 2).

Interestingly, the State Auditor's office also discovered a relationship between the commission's membership and the colleges they sanction. Between January 2009 and January 2014, only 2 of the 14 institutions that received a sanction had staff members on the commission. While this does not correlate to any wrongdoing per se, without an openly transparent forum in which to view the process of accreditation review there could be grounds for public and institutional skepticism about the efficacy —and ethicality —of the institution's decisions.

It is this lack of transparency combined with the concerns about an inability to produce new evidence when accreditation is revoked that prompted legal action against the ACCJC in 2014.

8.3.2   INSTITUTIONAL EVOLUTION

What lies beneath the ACCJC's evolving approach to institutional effectiveness is a growing concern for data-driven, evidence-based planning and operations. For example, strategic planning efforts have begun to focus on the disaggregation of student achievement metrics to catalyze equity-driven program review. When the climate is fertile for cultural change and there is a force to propel it, as has been the case in California with the ACCJC, true institutional evolution can begin to take place.

The epistemological roots of attitudinal shifts in community colleges toward evidence-based planning and effectiveness has many perspectives. Eaton (2007) explained that state and national government entities combined with accreditation commissions have been increasing pressure on community colleges to develop and implement systematic approaches to academic and operational planning, institutional decision-making, and program evaluation. By adopting such frameworks, Baker & Sax (2012) emphasized that higher education leaders can improve institutional effectiveness while latently improving student achievement goals, despite compliance with increasing demands by the Accrediting Commission for Community and Junior Colleges (ACCJC) making the process of institutional evolution challenging.

For any framework to be useful, it must be sensitive to institutional milieu. Organizations have a "cultural DNA" (Schein, 2004, p. 21) that requires sustained, productive momentum for any operational or administrative evolutionary process to occur. Tierney (1988) notes that this is especially true for colleges, and that all institutions of higher learning use a similar framework with which to construct that cultural DNA. In addressing the *how* of changing institutional culture, Bergquist (1992) goes a step further by developing out a conformable framework as a set of four cultural archetypes —collegial, managerial, developmental, and negotiating. Similarly, Kezar and Eckel (2002) purport that institutional evolution requires five components: support from senior administrators, collaborative leadership throughout the college, a robust evolution plan, proper staff development, and visibility of actions and their outcomes.

Bailey & Alfonso (2005) describe evolutionary processes as a shift from a culture of anecdotal analysis toward a culture of evidence. Institutions are encouraged to improve student achievement through the development, deployment, and assessment of empirically-based research instruments that then drive the institutional decision-making process. Just like how biological evolution is a whole-organism process, the successful integration of a metrics milieu requires full spectrum administrative and academic support, adequate enterprise resource planning, and enough time for the change process to take place.

Counter-attitudinal scholarship points to macro-level sampling in effectiveness studies when outlining how the rhetoric of institutional effectiveness evolution is not absolute. Skolits and Graybeal (2007) point out that local culture influences on institutional effectiveness are rarely presented nor accounted for, eluding to the necessity for more holistic, single-sample studies to approach institutional effectiveness change and administration with a phenomenological lens. However, a phenomenological approach —even with sensitivity to local culture —violates the statistical necessity for variations and quantity in sampling size for confident generalizations (Plummer, 1983).

8.3.3   TYING IT ALL TOGETHER

A foundational element that I have discovered in the literature on California community college accreditation by the ACCJC is an area of inquiry related to accreditation metrics. As it turns out, though the ACCJC enumerates guidelines for everything from financial planning integration to elements of a college's mission statement, the reliance on "qualitative opinions derived from quantitative data" (Roose & Anderson, 1972, p. 115) may render the process of self-evaluation as bias toward those institutions that have the resources and training necessary to produce or purchase rhetorically strong self-evaluation reports.

But accreditation metrics are only part of the issue. What lies beneath the ACCJC's evolving approach to institutional effectiveness is a growing concern for data-driven, evidence-based planning and operations. When climate is fertile for cultural change and there is a force to propel it, as has been the case in California, I describe this process as institutional evolution.

The epistemological roots of this attitudinal shift in community colleges toward evidence-based planning and effectiveness has many perspectives. Eaton (2007) explained that state and national government entities combined with accreditation commissions have been increasing pressure on community colleges to develop and implement systematic approaches to academic and operational planning, institutional decision-making, and program evaluation. By adopting such frameworks, Baker & Sax (2012) emphasized that higher education leaders can improve institutional effectiveness while latently improving student achievement goals, despite compliance with increasing demands by the Accrediting Commission for Community and Junior Colleges (ACCJC) making the process of institutional evolution challenging.

Organizations have a "cultural DNA" (Schein, 2004, p. 21) that requires sustained, productive momentum for any operational or administrative evolutionary process to occur. Tierney (1988) notes that this is especially true for colleges, and that all institutions of higher learning use a similar framework with which to construct that cultural DNA. Bergquist (1992) explains this conformable framework as a set of four cultural archetypes —collegial, managerial, developmental, and negotiating. Similarly, Kezar and Eckel (2002) purport that institutional evolution requires five components: support from senior administrators, collaborative leadership throughout the college, a robust evolution plan, proper staff development, and visibility of actions and their outcomes.

This evolutionary process is described by Bailey & Alfonso (2005) as a shift from a culture of anecdotal analysis toward a culture of evidence. Institutions are encouraged to improve student achievement through the development, deployment, and assessment of empirically-based research instruments that then drive the institutional decision-making process. Just like how biological evolution is a whole-organism process, the successful integration of a metrics milieu requires full spectrum administrative and academic support, adequate enterprise resource planning, and enough time for the change process to take place.

8.3.4 CLOSING THOUGHTS

The current process of accreditation serves not to measure but rather to explain, and without measurement there is no objective quantification of an institution's ability to meet its mission. How can we 1) define what an institution ought to do (i.e., what is their product), and 2) determine the best way to measure this? In contrast, is this an appropriate way to measure an institute of higher education?

My assumption here was that there is a desire to have a metric or even set of descriptive statistics with which a college can base their self-evaluation. This is somewhat eluded to in my field notes generated through discussions with institutional leaders. These grounded theory approaches to collecting data on accreditation preparedness has yielded three overarching themes: frustration with the inability of academic leaders to accurately predict accreditation strength; the recognition of accreditation in its current form as subjective and thus favoring those institutions that have the capacity and wherewithal to perform rigorous qualitative assessments; the desire for a wholly objective, peer-reviewed accreditation process that is separate from any one governing commission. All in all, this assumption has remained the same.

Additionally, as someone who works in research and technology in higher education, it is my assumption that all leaders are at least somewhat familiar with the data repositories that are provided to colleges and universities. It is also my assumption, however, that these repositories largely go under-utilized, as both experience and interview data has shown a disparity among the data collected and reported by institutions and the nature of college planning and program review. This alludes to an aspect of this topic that could have multiple interpretations, as what datasets should be used for what is highly debatable in many regards.

Data mining and knowledge discovery processes could help address the research challenges to accreditation planning. A central concern is whether there exists a set of aggregate quantitative data that could potentially facilitate a new accreditation preparedness metric. As I wrote before, there is a personal interest here for all those involved in institutional effectiveness because identifying a new metric for measuring an institution's ability to meet the needs of its community as an institution of higher education would greatly enhance the accreditation planning process. In my own personal job, I end up having to rely on professional judgment in accreditation planning rather than objective measures, turning the accreditation planning process into an exercise in forensics rather than a reporting process. This is a problem in colleges across the country, with leaders from different schools often times at odds when it comes to interpreting accreditation standards. It is in this research challenge that the connection between how to plan for accreditation, what data we currently use for accreditation, and what data we should use for accreditation is imputed. My assumptions here have not changed, either.

Finally, what constitutes an objective picture of an institution is fuzzily defined at best. While field notes have yielded conflicted opinions on what constitutes success in a higher education environment, most academic leaders have agreed that student outcomes, defined here as the relative grades and performance of college students, and student success, defined here as the attainment of institutional student goals (e.g., the conferral of a degree or certificate or the successful transfer to a 4-year university), are paramount to judging whether a college should be accredited or not. I share this opinion and I think this perspective will aid in the discovery of how a leader's perspectives on the accreditation process shape her or his college's strategic planning efforts and operations. The research I have dived into during this class have only helped to strengthen this resolve.

REFERENCES

Abdi, H. (2007). The method of least squares. In *Encyclopedia of Measurement and Statistics*. CA, USA: Thousand Oaks.

Age, L. J. (2011). Grounded Theory methodology: Positivism, hermeneutics, and pragmatism. *The Qualitative Report, 16*(6), 1599-1615.

Anguita, D., Ghelardoni, L., Ghio, A., Oneto, L., & Ridella, S. (2012, April). The 'K' in K-fold cross validation. Paper presented at the European Symposium on Artificial Neural Networks, Computational Intelligence, and Machine Learning, Bruges (Belgium).

Anscombe, F. (1961). Examination of residuals. *Proc. Fourth Berkeley Symp., 1,* 1-36.

Anscombe, F., & Tukey, J. (1963). The examination and analysis of residuals. *Technometrics, 5,* 141-160.

Areen, J. (2011). Accreditation reconsidered. *Iowa Law Review, 96*(5), 1471-1494.

Arlot, S., & Celisse, A. (2010). A survey of cross-validation procedures for model selection. *Statistics Surveys, 4,* 40-79.

Bailey, T. R., & Alfonso, M. (2005). *Paths to persistence: An analysis of research on program effectiveness at community colleges* (New Agenda series Volume 6, Number 1). Indianapolis, IN: Lumina

Foundation for Education.

Baker, J. H., & Sax, C. L. (2012). Building a culture of evidence: A case study of a California community college. *Journal of Applied Research in the Community College, 19*(2), 47-55.

Bergquist, W. H. (1992). *The four cultures of the academy: Insights and strategies for improving leadership in collegiate organizations.* San Francisco: Jossey-Bass.

Bickel, P. (1978). Using residuals robustly I: Tests for heteroscedasticity, nonlinearity. *Annals of Statistics, 6,* 266-291.

Bloland, H. G. (1999). Creating CHEA: Building a New National Organization on Accrediting. *The Journal of Higher Education, 70*(4), 357-388.

Brittingham, B. (2008). An uneasy partnership: accreditation and the Federal Government. *Change: The Magazine of Higher Learning, 40*(5), 32-38.

Burnham, K. P., & Anderson, D. R. (2004). Multimodel inference: Understanding AIC and BIC in model selection. *Sociological Methods & Research, 33*(2), 261-304.

California Community College Chancellor's Office (CCCCO). (2011). California Community College Chancellor's Office Website. Retrieved from http://www.cccco.edu

California State Auditor. (2014). California Community College Accreditation (Report 2013-123). Sacramento, CA.

Cohen, A. M., & Kisker, C. B. (2010). *The shaping of American higher education (2nd edition).* San Francisco: Jossey-Bass.

Cook, R., & Weisberg, S. (1983). Diagnostics for heteroscedasticity in regression. *Biometrika, 70,* 1-10.

Currie, K. (2009). Using survey data to assist theoretical sampling in grounded theory research. *Nurse Researcher, 17*(1), 24-33.

David, F. N. (1939). On Neyman's "smooth" test for goodness of fit. *Biometrika, 31*(1), 191-199.

Davidson, W. B., Beck, H. P., & Milligan, M. (2009). The college persistence questionnaire: Development and validation of an instrument that predicts student attrition. *Journal of College Student Development, 50*(4), 373-390.

Dechter, R., & Michie, D. (1985). *Structured induction of plans and programs* (Technical report). IBM Scientific Center, Los Angeles, CA.

Delen, D. (2010). A comparative analysis of machine learning techniques for student retention management. *Decision Support Systems, 49*, 498-506.

Denzin, N., & Lincoln, Y. S. (1994). *Handbook of Qualitative Research.* Thousand Oaks: Sage Publications.

Djulovic, A., & Li, D. (2013). Towards freshman retention prediction: A comparative study. International Journal of Information and Education Technology, 3(5), 494-500.

Dobson, A., & Barnett, A. (2008). *An introduction to generalized linear models, third edition.* Boca Raton: CRC Press.

Douglas, D. (2003). Grounded theories of management: A methodological review. *Management Research News, 26*, 44-60.

Dunne, C. (2011). The place of the literature review in grounded theory research. *International Journal of Social Research Methodology, 14*(2), 111-124.

Durkheim, E. (1951). *Suicide* (J. Spaulding & G. Simpson, trans.). Glencoe: The Free Press, 1961.

Eaton, J. (2007). Institutions, accreditors, and the federal government: redefining their "appropriate relationship." *Change, 39*(5), 16-23.

Eaton, J. (2011). U.S. accreditation: Meeting the challenges of accountability and student achievement. *Evaluation in Higher Education, 5*(1), 1-20.

Farrell, E. F. (2003). A common yardstick? the bush administration wants to standardize accreditation; educators say it is too complex for that. *The Chronicle of Higher Education, 49*(49), 25-26.

Fayyad, U., Piatetsky-Shapiro, G., & Smyth, P. (1996). From data mining to knowledge discovery in databases: an overview. In U. Fayad, G. Piatetsky-Shapiro, P. Smith, and R. Uthurusamy (Eds.), *Advances in Knowledge Discovery and Data Mining* (pp. 1-30). Menlo Park, CA: AAAI Press.

Fike, D. S., & Fike, R. (2008). Predictors of first-year student retention in the community college. *Community College Review, 36*(2), 68-88.

Fox, J. (2008). *Applied regression analysis and generalized linear models* (2nd edition). New York: Sage Publications.

Fox, J., & Weisberg, S. (2011). *An R companion to applied regression* (2nd edition). New York: Sage Publications.

Glaser, B.G. (1992). *Basics of Grounded Theory Analysis*. Mill Valley: Sociology Press.

Glaser, B. G. & Strauss, A. (1967). *The discovery of grounded theory: strategies for qualitative research*. Chicago: Aldine Publishing Company.

Golino, H. F., Gomes, C. M. A., & Andrade, D. (2014). Predicting academic achievement of high-school students using machine learning. *Psychology, 5*, 2046-2057.

Guan, J., Nunez, W., & Welsh, J. F. (2002). Institutional strategy and information support: the role of data warehousing in higher education. *Campus-Wide Information Systems, 19*(5), 168âĂŞ174.

Hand, D. J. (1981). *Discrimination and Classification*. Chichester, UK: Wiley.

Heise, David R. (1972). Employing nominal variables, induced variables, and block variables in path analysis. *Sociological Methods & Research, 1*(2), 147-173.

Hill, A. H. (1966). A longitudinal study of attrition among high aptitude college students. *Journal of Educational Research, 60*, 166-173.

Ioannidis, J. P. A. (2005). Why Most Published Research Findings Are False. *PLoS Medicine, 2*(8), e124.

Jain, A. K., & Dubes, R. C. (1988). *Algorithms for Clustering Data*. Englewood Cliffs, NJ: Prentice-Hall.

Jones, D. P. (2002). Different perspectives on information about educational quality: Implications for the role of accreditation. Washington, D. C.: Council for Higher Education Accreditation (CHEA).

Jones, R. & Noble, G. (2007). Grounded theory and management research: A lack of integrity? *Qualitative Research in Organizations and Management, 2*, 84-103.

Kezar, A, & Eckel, P. D. (2002). The effect of institutional culture on change strategies in higher education. *Journal of Higher Education, 73*(4), 435-460.

Knoell, D. M. (1960). Institutional research on retention and withdrawal. In H. T. Sprague (ed.), *Research on college students* (pp. 41-65). Boulder: Western Interstate Commission for Higher Education.

Kovacic, Z. J. (2012). Predicting student success by mining enrollment data. *Research in Higher Education Journal, 15*, 1-20.

Kuhn, M., & Johnson, K. (2013). *Applied predictive modeling.* New York: Springer.

Leef, G. C., & Burris, R. D. (2002). *Can college accreditation live up to its promise?* Washington, D.C.: American Council of Trustees and Alumni.

Liu, S., Gomez, J., Khan, B., & Yen, C. J. (2007). Toward a learner-oriented community college online course dropout framework. *International Journal on E-Learning, 6*(4), 519-542.

Locke, K. (1997). Re-writing the discovery of grounded theory after 25 years? *Journal of Management Inquiry, 5*, 239-245.

Locke, K. (2001). *Grounded theory in management research.* Thousand Oaks: Sage Publications.

Luan, J. (2002). Data mining and its applications in higher education. *New Directions for Institutional Research, 2002*(113), 17-36.

McClenney, K. M. (2004). Redefining quality in community colleges. *Change, 36*(6), 16-21.

Metz, G. W. (2005). Challenge and changes to TintoâÄŹs persistence theory: A historical review. *Journal of College Student Retention, 6*(2), 191-207.

Nandeshwar, A., Menzies, T., & Nelson, A. (2011). Learning patterns of university student retention. *Expert Systems with Applications, 38*, 14984-14996.

Neyman, J. (1937). Smooth "tes" for goodness of fit. *Skandinaviske Aktuarietidskrift, 20*, 150-199.

Nwosu, P. O., & Koller, J. (2014). Strategic planning and assessment in an outcomes-based funding environment. *Planning for Higher Education Journal, 42*(3), 58-72.

Park, C. L., Boman, J., Care, W. D., Edwards, M., & Perry, B. (2009).

Persistence and attrition: What is being measured? *Journal of College Student Retention, 10*(2), 223-233.

Pearson, K. (1900). On the criterion that a given system of deviations from the probable in the case of a correlated system of variables is such that it can be reasonably supposed to have arisen from random sampling. *Philosophical Magazine, 5*(L), 157-175.

Pena, E. A., & Slate, E. H. (2006). Global validation of linear model assumptions. *Journal of the American Statistical Association, 101*(473), 341-354.

Plummer, K. (1983). *Documents of life: An introduction to the problems and literature of a humanistic method.* London: Allen & Unwin.

Quinlan, J. R. (1986). Induction of decision trees. *Machine Learning, 1*, 81-106.

Roose, K. D., & Anderson, C. J. (1972). A rating of graduate programs. *Teachers College Record, 74*(1), 115-116.

Schein, E. H. (2004). *Organizational culture and leadership (3rd edition).* San Francisco: Jossey-Bass.

Shao, J. (1993). Linear model selection by cross-validation. *Journal of the American Statistical Association, 88*(422), 486-494.

Shibley, L. R., & Volkwein, J. F. (2002). Comparing the costs and benefits of re-accreditation processes. In *Comparing the Costs and Benefits of Re-Accreditation Processes. AIR 2002 Forum Paper.* Toronto, Ontario, Canada: Annual Meeting of the Association for Institutional Research.

Skolits, G. J., & Graybeal, S. Community college institutional effectiveness: perspectives of campus stakeholders. *Community College Review, 34*(4), 302-323.

Smaling, A. (2002). The argumentative quality of the qualitative research report. *International Journal of Qualitative Methods, 1*(3), 2-15.

Spiess, A. N., & Neumeyer, N. (2010). An evaluation of R2 as an inadequate measure for nonlinear models in pharmacological and biochemical research: a Monte Carlo approach. *BMC Pharmacology, 10*(6), 1-11.

Stern, P. N. (1994). Eroding grounded theory. In J. M. Morse (ed.), *Critical Issues in Qualitative Research Methods* (pp. 212-223). Thousand Oaks: Sage.

Strauss, A. L., & Corbin, J. (1990). *Basics of Qualitative Research: Grounded Theory Procedures and Techniques.* Thousand Oaks: Sage Publications.

Study Group on the Conditions of Excellence in Higher Education. (1984). *Involvement in college: Realizing the potential of American higher education.* A report of the National Institute of Education, U.S. Department of Education, Washington, DC: U.S. Government Printing Office.

Thomson, S. B. (2011). Sample size and Grounded Theory. *Journal of Administration and Governance, 5*(1), 45-52.

Tierney, W. G. (1988). Organizational culture in higher education: Defining the essentials. *Journal of Higher Education, 59*(1), 2-21.

Tinto, V. (1975). Dropout from higher education: A theoretical synthesis of recent research. *Review of Educational Research, 45*(1), 89-125.

Tinto, V. (2007). Research and practice of student retention: What's next? *Journal of College Student Retention: Research, Theory, & Practice, 8*(1), 1-19.

Vesey, W. B., Vesey, J. T., Stroter, A. D., & Middleton, K. V. (2011). Multiple linear regression: A return to basics in educational research. *Multiple Linear Regression Viewpoints, 37*(2), 14-22.

Wang, R., Chen, F., Chen, Z., Li, T., Harari, G., Tignor, S., Zhou, X., Ben-Zeev, D., & Campbell, A. T. (2014). StudentLife: Assessing mental health, academic performance and behavioral trends of college students using smartphones. Paper presented at Ubicomp '14 (September 13, 2014), Seattle, WA.

Western Association of Schools and Colleges' Accrediting Commission for Community and Junior Colleges (WASC-ACCJC). (2010). Western Association of Schools and Colleges' Accrediting Commission for Community and Junior Colleges (WASC-ACCJC) Website. Retrieved from http://www.accjc.org.

York, D. (1966). Least-Square Fitting of a Straight Line. *Canadian Journal of Physics, 44*, 1079-1086.

Zhang, H. (2004). The optimality of Naive Bayes. In: Proc. 17th International FLAIRS Conf., Florida, USA.

Made in the USA
Middletown, DE
30 March 2018